*The Inner Mirror*

# The Inner Mirror

*A-tri Dzogchen*

## Latri Khenpo Nyima Dakpa Rinpoche

Foreword by His Holiness, the 34th sMenri Trizin
Edited by Genyen Nyima Rangshar

**dream abbey**
PUBLISHING HOUSE

Dream Abbey
5551 2nd Ave S
Minneapolis, MN 55419 USA
dreamabbey.com

This paperback edition first published in 2019. Printed on acid-free paper.

Library of Congress Control Number:2019945910

ISBN 978-1-951105-00-6 (pbk.)
ISBN 978-1-951105-01-3 (ebook)

# Contents

Tonpa Shenrab - The Enlightened One
Founder of Bön

# Foreword

*By His Holiness, the 34<sup>th</sup> sMenri Trizin, worldwide spiritual leader of the Bön religion.*

In recent years there has been a great increase worldwide in spiritual values, inner transformation, and improving the quality of our mind. The global interest in mindfulness and related practices, whether yoga, meditation or more formal religious practice, demonstrates the human need for improvement in our inner, spiritual lives. Yungdrung Bön's 18,000-year spiritual tradition has always been present for those who want to use it for their own personal spiritual development and to help others.

Now it is even more important that Bön teachings be available to people worldwide, and essential to have important Bön texts available in English for a worldwide audience of spiritual seekers.

For this reason, Latri Nyima Dakpa Rinpoche has written this book, an explanation and commentary on the Fifteen-Session A-tri Dzogchen text. This text is a key text in the Dzogchen cycle of teachings. Dzogchen is the highest of the Bön teachings, and is crucial for understanding and improving our mind.

Latri Nyima Dakpa Rinpoche, a senior Rinpoche at sMenri Monastery, has taught Dzogchen and other Bön teachings worldwide for over thirty years. Rinpoche is a dynamic speaker and teacher who has a keen ability to touch the hearts of his students. Now Rinpoche has written this book in a clear, understandable way that makes these important teachings more accessible to Western practitioners.

I am pleased with Rinpoche's hard work and dedication in writing this book, and I trust that this book will be helpful to many practitioners to implement these important teachings in their practice.

With my blessings and prayers,

*sMenri Trizin Lungtok Dawa Dhargyal*

## ༈ རྒྱལ་བ་གཡུང་དྲུང་བོན་གྱི་རྗེ་གཉིས་ཤེལ། ༈

**His Holiness The 34ᵗʰ Gyalwa Menri Trizin**

Date: 24/07/2018

# Forward

In recent years there has been a great increase worldwide in spiritual values, inner transformation, and improving the quality of our mind. The global interest in mindfulness and related practices, whether yoga, meditation or more formal religious practice, demonstrates the human need for improvement in our inner, spiritual lives. Yungdrung Bön's 18,000-year spiritual tradition has always been present for those who want to use it for their own personal spiritual development and to help others.

Now it is even more important that Bön teachings be available to people worldwide, and essential to have important Bön texts available in English for a worldwide audience of spiritual seekers.

For this reason, Latri Nyima Dakpa Rinpoche has written this book, an explanation and commentary on the 15 Session A-Tri Dzogchen text. This text is a key text in the Dzogchen cycle of teachings. Dzogchen is the highest of the Bön teachings, and is crucial for understanding and improving our mind.

Latri Nyima Dakpa Rinpoche, a senior Rinpoche at sMenri Monastery, has taught Dzogchen and other Bön teachings worldwide for over 30 years. Rinpoche is a dynamic speaker and teacher who has a keen ability to touch the hearts of his students. Now Rinpoche has written this book in a clear, understandable way that makes these important teachings more accessible to Western practitioners.

I am pleased with Rinpoche's hard work and dedication in writing this book, and I trust that this book will be helpful to many practitioners to implement these important teachings in their practice.

With my blessings and prayers,

sMenri Trizin Lungtok Dawa Dhargyal

---

Menri Monastery, P.O. Kotla Panjola, Oachghat, Solan -173223, Himachal Pradesh, INDIA
E-mail: menritrizin@rediffmail.com

# Acknowledgement

Many years of time and effort went into creating this book, *The Inner Mirror*, based on the Fifteen Sessions of the A-tri tradition of Dzogchen. I wrote this book in many places, during my travels to teach Bön to my students in the West. Many students were able to learn about Bön from my previous book, *Opening the Door to Bön*. *The Inner Mirror* will allow these students to deepen their knowledge and experience of the practice and learn advanced Dzogchen teachings.

I am thankful to many people who have been instrumental in helping me with this book. Without their inspiration and continued support, this book would not have become a reality.

I would like to thank to my center in Poland, and the Audio Committee of Sharza Ling Institute, for recording my several years of teaching of the Fifteen Sessions of A-tri Dzogchen, on which this book is based. I thank them also for all the other work they have done to help me bring Bön to my students.

I thank my student from Ukraine, Maya Samara, who transcribed the recordings to make the first transcription of this book. Her pure dedication and hard work created a genuine and meaningful contribution to this book.

My thanks go to Eleanor Capanegro, my student in Santa Fe, New Mexico, for her help with the artwork for this book.

I also thank my student Nick Tichawa, the current Umdze of Yeru Bön Center, for all his time and assistance, particularly with the final proofing and assembly of the book.

I wish to express my heartfelt thanks to my long-time serious student, David Peteler, who helped with editing and proofing this book and providing suggestions to make this book even more valuable. He and his wife Deborah Peteler have encouraged me all the time, in all of my work, and especially on this book. Whenever I needed anything, they have always been there, with no questions. From the core of my heart, I thank you both with great appreciation.

I am especially grateful to Deborah Peteler, who was my strong backbone on this book, for her encouragement, her help with obtaining all the materials I needed, and her forceful enthusiasm and encouragement to help me complete this book. I also thank her for her kind help in designing the cover of this book. And I am grateful to her ongoing support of Yeru Bön Center as well as her family.

I thank all of those who have been part of this book in many ways, even though their names are not mentioned here.

Finally, I dedicate all the merit received from this book to all supporters and people on the earth for peace and harmony; to the long duration of the Dzogchen wisdom. May this book be the cause of readers to reach the final attainment of rainbow body.

*Latri Khenpo Nyima Dakpa*

# Introduction to A-tri Dzogchen

Tonpa Shenrab, the Enlightened One and founder of Bön, gave the teachings of Bön to mankind. These teachings, known as The Nine Ways of Bön, are well known. Also commonly known are the Three Transmissions of Bön, which are outer, inner, and secret.

The outer transmission (*chi gyud*) is transmitted through the manifestation body (*tulku*) of the Enlightened One. The inner transmission (*nang gyud*) is transmitted through the perfection body (*dzogku*). The secret transmission (*sang gyud*) is transmitted through the Primordial Enlightened One (*bönku*). The secret transmission has three main traditions, which are the teachings on *A-tri*, the *Zhangzhung Nyengyud*, and *Dzogchen*. Among these traditions, this book belongs to the A-tri tradition.

In the eighth century, the Buddhists came from India to Tibet. Yungdrung Bön, the root of the Tibetan culture, religion, and language, was discriminated against and put in the position of almost losing its identity; particularly at risk were the highly developed traditions of these practices. They remained almost in name only. During this crisis time, when it was needed most, The Great Hermit (Gongzoed Ritrod Chenpo, 1038–1096), revived the A-tri teaching system. Ritrod Chenpo is known as the Great Preserver of these experiential teachings, and his work was like that of the Enlightened One appearing in human form. The Great Hermit's three great accomplishments were to revive the dying experiential transmission (*nyam gyud*) hermit tradition, by creating an *A-tri Dzogchen* practice manual for the sake of all sentient beings; preserving the hermit system of meditation; and training and educating a new generation of practitioners to carry on the lineage of this tradition.

Ritrod Chenpo created the A-tri practice manual based on the Dzogchen series of teachings, which was directly transmitted by Kungtu Zangpo, and also the texts known as *The Nine Circles of the Hidden Enlightened Mind* (*Jang Sem Gappa Gukor*), *The Ninefold Lower Mind* (*Sem Mad Dhe Gu*), and also his own mind-treasury from his personal practice of Dzogchen.

Later on, the great Dzogchen master Yorpo Mepal (1134–1168), the successor of The Great Hermit, revised and clarified Ritrod Chenpo's work into an *Eighty-Session A-tri Dzogchen* text, which became the foundation of the entire A-tri tradition. Drogon Ladoe Gyaltsen (1198–1263) condensed this text from eighty sessions into thirty sessions. After that, Dru Gyalwa Yungdrung (1242–1290) condensed it further into the current *Fifteen-Session A-tri of Yeru*, which we use today.

The above is a very general introduction of the *A-tri* tradition. This book is based on the *Fifteen-Session A-tri*, which I have explained in great detail. I have received all the teachings of Bön, the outer, inner and secret, from the late His Holiness 33rd sMenri Trizin and His Eminence Yongzin Rinpoche. From 1990 until now, I have traveled in the Western world, even in places where they have not heard about Bön in the past. Based on the desire and needs of the students there, I have offered the teachings of Bön, and have planted the seeds of Yungdrung Bön in their lives. By introducing Bön to them, I have established positive karma in their lives. Among these students, some have developed exceptional experience and deep understanding of Dzogchen. Many of the devotees and practitioners have achieved significant spiritual development.

My hope for the future is that this book may contribute to the tradition of Yungdrung Bön teaching, and in particular may help to preserve and expand the Dzogchen teaching. I dedicate this book to my most kind root teachers, the late HH 33rd sMenri Trizin Rinpoche, His Eminence Yongzin Rinpoche, and Lharampa Geshe Tsundue Gongphel (Yungdrung Namgyal), as an offering to them in appreciation for their great kindness to me. In addition, any merit I have collected through this action I dedicate to Yungdrung Bön and wish that all sentient beings may benefit from it.

*Latri Khenpo Nyima Dakpa Rinpoche*

# Editor's Introduction

This book is based on a series of teachings and commentary by Rinpoche on several Dzogchen texts, particularly the text, *Fifteen Sessions of A-tri Dzogchen*. Rinpoche gave these teachings and commentaries to his students over the course of several years in several different locations, including Shardza Ling in Poznan, Poland; Shenchen Ling in Minsk, Byelorus; and Yeru Bön Center in Minneapolis and Los Angeles. Rinpoche gave these lectures in English. These lessons were transcribed by devoted students and have been revised, edited, and presented in this volume.

The teachings are structured on the organization of the Fifteen-Session A-tri Dzogchen text. They begin with the *ngondro* and cover the *ngozhi* through to the *je kyi chawa*.

Because this book is based on these oral teachings and commentary, it is not written in the style of a rigorous academic treatise. Rather, it explains the principles of Dzogchen in the conversational speech and tone of Rinpoche, a master at communicating complicated Bön teachings to lay, and particularly Western, audiences. This is a continuation of the ancient tradition of the master passing knowledge down to the disciples from mouth to ear.

Bön teaches that no one attains enlightenment without the aid of a great teacher. This is an opportunity to learn a seminal Dzogchen text from a great master. Readers should enjoy the direct, conversational transmission of this great wisdom, delivered with compassion and humor by a great, modern Bön master. Practitioners should follow the instructions of this text, practice enthusiastically, and seek the guidance of a true Dzogchen master such as Rinpoche to help guide their practice.

*Mu tsug marro!*

*Genyen Nyima Rangshar*

# Introduction

# About A-tri Dzogchen

Dzogchen is considered the highest teaching in the Bön tradition. *Dzogchen* is made up of two words: *dzog*, meaning "perfect" or "complete;" and *chen*, meaning "great, limitless." Dzogchen, the Great Perfection, teaches that everything is perfect and complete within the natural state.

In Bön, there are three Dzogchen traditions or lineages. These are known as *A-tri, Zhangzhung Nyengyud,* and *Dzogchen.* They come from different sources; they have slightly different ways of teaching; and at a deep level, they have slight differences. But in their essence they are not different from each other.

This book discusses a set of teachings according to the *A-tri* tradition, known as the *Fifteen Sessions of A-tri.* During the persecution of Bön in the eighth century, many texts of Bön teachings (called "treasures") were hidden. They were rediscovered in the eleventh century, mainly by Shenchen Luga, one of the great masters from Tonpa Shenrab's clan. In the eleventh century Gongdzo Ritro Chenpo, a disciple of Shenchen Luga, revived the experiential hermit transmission system. Based on his own personal knowledge from this experiential transmission system, he created a practice manual which was the seed of the A-tri system. He systematized these teachings into 80 sessions. Gradually, the text was shortened to 30 sessions by other masters.

Dru Gyalwa Yungdrung, in the thirteenth century, was one of the masters from the Dru lineage and an important master of the Yeru Wensaka tradition. Yeru Wensaka was the main center of Bön education in those times, after the rehabilitation of Bön from the persecutions. Dru Gyalwa Yungdrung condensed the thirty sessions into fifteen sessions, based on his own experience and the teachings he received from his teachers. The teaching was thereafter known as "The Great A-tri of the Dru lineage."

The fifteen sessions contain three main sections. The first section is the *ngondro*, or preliminary (foundation) practice. The ngondro practice awakens the state of awareness that is not yet awakened. The second section is the *ngozhi*, the main practice. The ngozhi practice develops what was awakened. The third section is achieving liberation as the accomplishment of our practice.

The first section, the ngondro, is divided into four parts. The first part is the practice of impermanence, which is done to reverse the attachment to *khorwa*, (cyclic existence; Sanskrit *samsara*). The second part is the practice of refuge and of the mind of enlightenment, which opens the door of the path to enlightenment. The third part is the practice of the offering of the mandala. The mandala offering practice is done to cultivate two kinds of merit: the merit of method or compassion, and the merit of wisdom. The fourth part is the practice of *lamé naljor*, the supplication prayer to the lama, which we practice in order to discover self-realization and receive blessings.

# How To Practice

## The Correct View of Practice

Starting right now, we all have to generate a pure attitude towards the teachings and our practice. Of course, we all are very busy. But at least during our practice time and during teachings, we have to be calm, genuine, and sincere about the practice. The main thing is to create a harmonious environment and to dedicate each moment to practice. During practice time and teachings, we should generate a pure attitude and dedication. This pure attitude and dedication is always necessary, from the first day of the preliminary practices until we achieve enlightenment. The pure attitude and dedication are important because our mind is most important, and a pure attitude makes a difference in the results of the actions of body, speech, and mind.

We all attend teaching sessions with certain expectations and hopes. You come here to learn and to practice. I come here to teach, to share my knowledge and experiences, to share the teachings I have received from my teachers. How much you receive from what I give depends on how you receive it—how focused and aware you are. Therefore, we must not waste time and energy. The essence of practice lies in the knowledge of how to apply the teachings where they are necessary. If our intentions are not pure, if we receive teachings with negative intentions and a competitive attitude towards our friends and fellow students, then we are only wasting our time.

The purpose of these teachings is to develop our mind in the proper direction. If our mind stays the same as it was, it means we are not properly applying our practice, so we receive no benefit. Our teacher can only wish us well and pray that these teachings benefit students by the blessings of Tonpa Shenrab and of our root teachers. The rest is in our hands. If you are not ready to change, then even if Tonpa Shenrab came here, he would not be able to do anything. That's why we, all sentient beings, are the same as we were when he was here—unliberated, untransformed, unchanged, full of poisons, ignorance, egoism, and still suffering in khorwa.

If this could only be changed by the blessings of great enlightened ones, Tonpa Shenrab, Chamma, Yeshe Walmo, realized teachers who would do everything to liberate all sentient beings, then no sentient being would suffer in khorwa at this moment. These great realized teachers did all they could do. They taught us the lowest way of the *dho* (Sanskrit *sutra*) to give us a chance and see how we would do. Then gradually they tried a different way, hoping that it would help us, and taught us *ngag* (Sanskrit *tantra*). At last, they gave us the highest level of teachings, which lead to complete liberation by teaching us Dzogchen. But only a very small number of us have benefited from them and achieved enlightenment. Why? It's not because the enlightened masters lack compassion or wisdom. It's because we lack sufficient effort and dedication to practice in the way they taught us. So, we cannot complain about those great masters and enlightened ones. We should complain about ourselves and correct ourselves.

We begin correcting ourselves from our mind. How do we change and correct our mind, our attitude? There are two ways to correct our inner negative thinking. The first is according to the enlightened mind of the *yungdrung sempa* (Sanskrit *bodhisattva*), and the second is the pure vision according to ngag.

Ngag teaches that we should not view our surroundings in the ordinary way. Instead of thinking of our surroundings as a simple room, we should imagine them as a pure, spiritual, enlightened land. We should listen to the teachings as not just the speech of our human teacher, but the real speech of Sanggye Tonpa Shenrab. We should view our teacher not as an ordinary person, but as the real form of Tonpa Shenrab, Drenpa Namkha or Shenlha Ökar. We should think that the teacher is an enlightened being, inseparable from the *Sanggye* (Enlightened One; Sanskrit *Buddha*). We should view our fellow practitioners as *khadros* and *rigdzins*, enlightened women and realized tantric practitioners (*ngag gi naljorpa*). It does not mean that our fellow practitioners have to be realized yogis. If they aren't, it doesn't matter. The important thing is how we view them. The way we think about others must be pure and free from negativity. Once we are able to view others in that way, it means that we are developing the correct understanding and the pure, non-negative view. It is important that we train ourselves to perceive things in a positive way.

In Tibet, we have a saying: when we talk about important things, we must be very precise and repeat them a hundred times, to continually remind ourselves. We know many things, and we generally understand them, but we don't truly realize them. Understanding is different from realization. Understanding doesn't mean that we have realized anything. We must truly realize things at a deep level.

When we talk about the mind, each of us has a different definition, but we all understand what mind I'm talking about, although we haven't realized that mind. We have heard about enlightenment and Buddhahood a thousand times, but still we haven't discovered and fully understood what Sanggye really is and what his qualities are. It's the same with suffering and khorwa. We often talk about khorwa in our daily life, and we frequently talk about the suffering of khorwa. But as soon as we finish the conversation about the suffering of khorwa, we forget about it. We have no realization or inner awareness of the suffering of khorwa. We have a little information about khorwa, but we haven't truly realized it.

## Incorrect Attitudes Towards the Teachings

Whenever we prepare any ceremony or receive teachings or empowerments, it is very important to first generate a pure, genuine, good attitude and motivation. The result of most actions depends on our thoughts and motivation, on the attitude we assume. When we receive teachings or empowerments or do practice, we need to have the correct attitude, a pure attitude and pure motivation, in order to receive the teachings and blessings.

A Bön practitioner must do three things. The first is *thoepa*, listening to the teaching. The second is *sampa*, reflecting or thinking about the teaching. The third is *gompa*, meditating on the teaching to realize it.

## Three Faults of the Container

According to the root ngag of Chamma, the Loving Mother, the "Three Faults of the Container" are: (i) a pot that is upside down; (ii) a pot that has a hole in the bottom; and (iii) a pot that has poison in it.

When your mind consciousness and ear consciousness are not present and attentive in class, then no matter what the teacher delivers or how precious the teachings are, your ear consciousness doesn't receive them. We are like a pot placed upside down under running water. If we want to fill the pot with water, we need to place it right side up, so it can hold the water. If our body is sitting in class but our mind is wandering somewhere else, then our ear consciousness is not receiving the teachings. That is like bringing a dog into the teaching session. The dog may hear some sounds, but he will not grasp the meaning of what he hears. The wisdom opposite of this first fault is when we are listening carefully, word by word, to what the teacher says.

The second fault is a pot that has a hole in the bottom. Although it is right side up, it's leaking, and it cannot hold any water. No matter how much water we put into it, the water leaks out. So even though you may hear some teachings through your ear consciousness, your mind consciousness doesn't retain them. Because we don't retain anything in our mind, we can't reflect on it or practice it.

The third fault is a pot with poison in it. You can listen to the teachings attentively and hold what you've heard in your mind. But if you have a negative attitude, such as an attitude of competitiveness with other students, anger, or jealousy, it's like poison in the pot. If you keep food in a pot with poison, even though the pot is beautiful, and the food is delicious, the food will bring no benefit to you or others. If you have received teachings, but you keep them with an attitude of anger or jealousy, or with the hope of gaining fame and good reputation, you are receiving these precious teachings with the wrong attitude. They will not bring benefit to you or others.

We should all meditate to see if we have any of these faults. When we find that we have one or more of these faults, we have to change our attitude. This is very important; otherwise we are wasting our time and opportunity. If we have these faults, then the teaching will not be able to help us. Your teacher will not be able to help. Tonpa Shenrab will not be able to help. As long as our attitude is wrong, our mind is poisoned, and nothing will help.

One example of the poison of negative attitudes comes from the early history of Tonpa Shenrab's life, described in his biography. A prince came to one of Tonpa Shenrab's teachings. This prince was one of the most sinful people in that area. He was very violent, full of anger and jealousy. When Tonpa Shenrab taught and the prince attended the session, only his physical body was present there. Mentally, he was projecting all sorts of his violent activities and assuming negative attitudes. Tonpa Shenrab could not help him. His teachings could not heal him or correct him. He wasn't ready to receive them. Nothing of the teachings was transmitted into him, because his mind was filled with negativity.

We mustn't be like that. Each of us must have pure motivation. Look within yourself and ask, why are you reading this book? Do you have any of these faults? If you do, you should correct them, and come back to where your body is.

I also pray and seek blessings from Tonpa Shenrab and other great spiritual masters, and directly from my teachers, that I can be of benefit to all of you, and that I may deliver the teachings in a pure and perfect way. This advice is important not only for the disciple, but also for the teacher.

# PART I

# Ngondro

# Meditation on Impermanence

The session is dedicated to ngondro. The first part of this session is meditation on impermanence. Why is it the first practice? Because it is important that we develop a true, inner realization of impermanence. Without the inner realization of impermanence, we will probably not engage enthusiastically in practice. If we understand the unstable and changing nature of all phenomena, we will be motivated to practice.

Many of us have an attitude of postponing our practice. We think, maybe we will do it tomorrow, next evening, next month, or next year. That's the process we automatically follow. We believe that we can do what we want, that we can plan for the next day, month, or year. But in reality, the future is not certain. Time is not in our hands. Our death is with us from the time we are born. Only the time, place, and conditions of death are not certain. We are fortunate to have perfect human conditions, knowledge, health, but these conditions are all changeable, transformable. Ultimately, these conditions will change and be destroyed, and we will die.

If we think from this perspective, then we should not postpone our practice for later. All the conditions we have now, what we are now, how we are now, where we are now, are changing and getting destroyed every minute, no matter what our expectations are. The Tibetan word for impermanence is *mitakpa*, meaning nothing is everlasting, permanent, or solid. We should take advantage of those temporarily occurring conditions while they last. Therefore, the early masters practiced impermanence as the first step. Once you receive these teachings, normally you should practice them for a week or ten days, doing four or six sessions a day. You should engage in this practice to experience and feel what our condition is.

We humans are very self-centered. Our grasping and self-centeredness is also impermanent. It also transforms and changes. Our self is not inherently solid; we just think it is. It exists only in this very moment. There are many examples that we can use to practice and many ways and methods we can apply as a support to help realize impermanence. Just saying and knowing that we are impermanent, changing, and transforming, is not helpful. We know this on an intellectual level, but we need to realize it at a deep, emotional level, and to apply and practice it. Then we will benefit from it.

The main theme of this practice is to think that, while we have such a wonderful, perfect opportunity for practice, we mustn't waste it. We must use it to our advantage and benefit from it, realize the Bön teachings deeply, and follow the path to enlightenment.

Reflect on yourself right now. If you were about to die right now, what would you have to carry with you? Do you have anything for your benefit in the *bardo*, the intermediate state? All our material things, our relatives, parents, and friends will not be helpful, because we cannot carry them with us.

Reflect on the changes happening in the world. We can see how the universe itself is transforming: changes in the climate, financial condition of the countries, the health of the planet and people. You can find many examples in the news of a wealthy, successful individual or family, who had a wonderful, privileged life, a life of luxury, but were killed by an unfortunate accident. Despite their earlier status, their conditions changed, unexpected conditions appeared, death appeared, and their situation changed completely.

If that was you, if that was me, what would I have to carry to help in the process of dying, in the process of rebirth? What do we have? We should put ourselves in the place of those who are suffering, going through changes, transforming. And then think, if that were me, what would I experience, what would I have?

We should reflect on things that can give us a faster and deeper understanding and realization of impermanence. Bön masters in early times often went to cemeteries to see dead bodies and skeletons, reflect on them, and put themselves in their place. They thought about how those people had passed and changed to skeletons, to a handful of ash. We use these examples, and in each session we try to meditate on impermanence, and to really experience it.

We should also think that our end is death. Of this we are certain. And death will follow its own way. Nobody can save our life, and nobody can help us on the way except for ourselves. None of the wealth we accumulated in our lifetime, none of our family members, nothing can help us except our practice. At the time of our death, we can only remember the teachings, remember the teacher, the Sanggye, we can take refuge, and realize that we go empty-handed. We can also meditate on the quality of impermanence of the past Sanggye, the past great masters. Some of them had complete power to live as long as they wished, and had complete power to transform other beings; but they also followed the path of impermanence. They submitted to the same conditions that rule us.

I'm not trying to emphasize that we will die. The main aim of this practice of impermanence is to show you why you should engage in practice without postponing it. We all have a strong concept of our own permanence. We think we will still be here next week, next year, the next few more years. We must realize that this strong concept, shared by all human beings, is false. We need to transform this concept through practice. We should not waste time.

When we truly realize impermanence, we should apply this new attitude in our real life, as our real quality. Then every moment of our life will be more meaningful. We will engage in practice more. If we think of our daily life and spirituality as two separate, unrelated areas, we are wrong. Our daily life and spirituality have to be brought together. One has to benefit from the other. We should learn to apply our practice in every moment of our daily life and benefit from it.

If we continuously engage in this practice and put a little more effort into it, then after some time we will experience how much we have understood and realized this practice. That inner realization will change the way we see all existing phenomena. We will see all phenomena, all the material world, as essenceless, truthless, as an illusion. When the thought of our own permanence arises, if we can detach from the attachment and grasping that we had before, if the attachment and grasping get weaker, that is a sign that we have benefited from this practice.

This text says that after continuous practice, we will experience greater detachment from this existing, material world, and we will realize that all phenomena are transforming from moment to moment. We will realize it spontaneously, without any special effort. We will know it like we remember our name or our mother and father—without any effort. If we always have that kind of feeling, this is an inner sign that we have achieved the deep understanding of impermanence.

The concept of friend and enemy is naturally cut off by the power of this practice. We will remember the Bön teachings, will always engage in practice, and will try to benefit other beings. This attitude will spontaneously arise in us, without need for any effort or thoughts. The text quotes a lama who says, "Once you are born, it's definitely sure that you will die. Once you die, it's definitely sure that you will be reborn. Once you are reborn, you will again circulate in khorwa. All this is essenceless. Your circulation in khorwa bears no fruit, but you still do so." And he continues, "So all you students, all you fortunate practitioners, realize that khorwa has no essence. Can you see it? It's time for you to awaken and realize the nature of impermanence."

## A Meditation on Impermanence

Let's do a meditation and reflect on the teaching of this session, so the teaching doesn't remain just words or notes in your books.

Sit comfortably, in the cross-legged position if you can. Cross your legs, rest your hands on your lap in meditation position, with the right hand underneath the left, thumbs touching the base of the ring fingers. Straighten your spine. Open your shoulders, like an eagle ready to take off from earth. Keep your neck in a normal position, without bending it up or down.

Now think about the people buried in a cemetery, about those who have died and who were healthy, had a family, led a happy, comfortable life like we do, but nevertheless have passed away. Or think of changes going on in other countries. Think about whatever makes it easy for you to understand impermanence. Try to put yourself in the position of people going through changes and try to feel and understand their experience. You are also subject to impermanence, and you will go through similar changes.

We have to do this kind of practice every day. If we are busy, we should at least think about it and practice it in the morning and in the evening. It motivates us to engage in the practice, and when we practice, we expand our realization, experience, and wisdom. It's easy to use the smallest reasons as an excuse to postpone our practice. We all know this from personal experience. Without understanding the nature of impermanence, you will not have a strong motivation to become a strong practitioner.

As I mentioned, the early Bön masters practiced impermanence as their first meditation for a reason. Often, practitioners would write on their wall "Life is impermanent," "Remember impermanence," "Contemplate the natural state of mind," or "Be aware of the *rigpa*." They put those signs in their house, so when they saw them, they were reminded to do impermanence practice. Early masters sometimes put a skeleton or some bones in the entrance door to their house, so every time they walked in or out, they were reminded of their death. This reminded them to practice; "Oh, yes, the same thing will happen to me. I will be in same condition. I must utilize this moment of my life to practice."

This is the end of the part on impermanence practice. Practice impermanence as a starting point to enter the teachings and to begin the pathway to enlightenment. The text says we should practice it for five or seven days.

# Generating the Mind of Enlightenment; Taking Refuge

The second part of the ngondro is known as "generating the mind of enlightenment" and "taking refuge." The teachings on *semkyed* (generating the mind of enlightenment), come before those on *kyabdro* (taking refuge). Usually we talk first about kyabdro, taking refuge, and then about semkyed, generating the mind of enlightenment. But in the A-tri ngondro, the text teaches semkyed, the mind of enlightenment, first. It's important to practice both, no matter which is first. As we discussed earlier, the most important thing is our attitude of mind. Our attitude of mind determines what we will generate. With the proper attitude of mind, we will get the appropriate results. We should generate a pure attitude of goodwill to other beings, and we should practice to benefit all sentient beings.

## Compassion and Generating the Mind of Enlightenment

Generating the mind of enlightenment and taking refuge are two different fields of practice. They arise due to two different causes. The semkyed is based more on compassion, because only compassion can lead us to generate the mind of enlightenment. Without compassion, we would have no reason to generate the mind of enlightenment. The main attitude, aim, and action of generating the mind of enlightenment is to completely take responsibility and dedicate yourself, devote yourself to practice to generate the mind of enlightenment, in order to benefit sentient beings and liberate them from khorwa. For this purpose, we practice to achieve enlightenment.

How do we generate compassion? When everything is going well, life is perfect and we are happy, we don't feel the urge to be compassionate. When someone is in a condition equal to ours, there is no reason to generate compassion. Compassion arises when we notice, looking from our perspective, that others are suffering more than we are; that they are experiencing more sorrowful, more unpleasant, poorer, and weaker conditions. Only then can we generate compassion. The compassion we refer to here is based on the suffering of khorwa, of this existing world, to which we are all bound. We're under its dictate and influence, according to our own condition of suffering, dissatisfaction, and unhappiness. Even though we have a reason or excuse to complain, still we cannot overcome khorwa. We continue to circle in it.

We have been circling in this cyclic world for countless lifetimes. Through these countless lifetimes, all sentient beings once were our parents, mothers, fathers, and children. We should generate the understanding of this fact and transform all sentient beings, seeing them as our parents or children. Then, we should look at the example of our parents in this present life, how they were kind to us, cared for us, loved us. All sentient beings equally expect to enjoy happiness and good care, good conditions for themselves, as we expect it for ourselves. None of us expect to experience miserable conditions of life, suffering, and unhappiness. We all desire happiness and joy. But we keep creating the unhappiness and unpleasant conditions for ourselves, because we don't understand the real sources of what we create. In every moment, the actions we take through our body, mind, and speech are creating those conditions. We create our own unhappiness. And we should have compassion for others who are not aware of this source of suffering, and therefore do not have the ability to heal it.

It's not easy to generate compassion to all sentient beings. First, we should understand the real source of suffering of each and every person. Then, we begin to transform it on larger groups, villages, communities, and countries. That's the way to practice it. To practice compassion, we first have to realize "equanimity," meaning that each and every one of us is equal.

## Tsad Med Zhi: The Four Measureless Practice

The mind of enlightenment holds the perfection of the four measureless qualities, which are measureless compassion, measureless kindness, measureless love, and measureless equanimity. "Measureless" indicates that these qualities are boundless, with no limit; it is our khorwa-mind that wants to put limits on these qualities.

When we talk about the four measureless qualities, we put compassion first, then kindness, love, and equanimity. But when we practice them we need to start from equanimity, then move to happiness, then kindness, and then compassion for the suffering of sentient beings.

### Tang Nyom: Equanimity

The first step is called *tang nyom*, the "equanimity" of self and others. The mind of compassion views others as equal with ourselves. Normally we are not equal, because in every choice that we make we choose to care for ourselves first, to protect and secure ourselves, because our self is most important to us. Only when we see there's a chance to do something for others without losing anything for ourselves, then we might start to care for all that is "mine:" my friend, my family, my mother, my father. Always, directly and indirectly, our self is involved, connected with what we care for. Our self is always present. We are self-minded and self-grasping. We must decrease this concept of self-mindedness and self-grasping, so that we can respect and understand others.

28

We should understand that we had a mother and child relationship with all sentient beings. With that attitude, we begin to reduce our view of our own self-importance. Instead, we should view ourselves and others as equals and care equally for others as we do for us. When we begin to understand ourselves and others as equal, we start to practice this level of understanding on a regular basis. After some time and practice, we should develop the understanding of the equality of ourselves and others without having to think about our relationship as mother and child, etc. We immediately think that we are equal with others. We have this thought without any difficulty—without any effort needed.

## Gawa: Joy

Then we can go to the next step, called *gawa*, meaning "sharing joy." We wish happiness, joy, and pleasure for others. We should generate the attitude that we enjoy and appreciate the qualities and goodwill of others. We should generate this attitude to all sentient beings. How great will your joy and happiness be when you get something marvelous, some good results in your business, job, practice? Everything that makes you happy and gives you joy should be accepted with goodwill. This attitude of happiness, joy, and appreciation should be generated for others. We have to practice *gawa* until we can experience it spontaneously, without any problem, without any need for reflecting on gradual steps. Then immediately, when something good happens, not even to your friend or parents, but even people whom you dislike, we should appreciate it and feel happy about it. They deserve good things, too, even when we don't favor these people. We should think about how much we would appreciate it if we were in their place. Why? Because you appreciate it when good things happen to you. Why not be happy for others too? For them it's their selves. The self is the self. We need to give up the self-minded attitude, change it, and feel for others the joy that we would feel in their place and accept their joy. This is *gawa*, joy.

## Jampa: Kindness

The third step is "kindness" towards all sentient beings, called *jampa*. Kindness comes now, because when we have understood the equal importance of ourselves and others, we should also treat them with kindness and love, just as we appreciate being treated with love and kindness. If someone is kind to us, how do we feel? What do we experience? Others feel the same way, and they have the same right to it as we do. So we have to be more kind and loving towards all sentient beings. We have to practice that.

It's not easy to generate that attitude. Sometimes we think, "Today I will do one practice, and tomorrow I will jump to another," but that's not a good way. If we want to experience the effects of our practice, we have to keep doing them until the results occur and we get the experience. Then you also have a chance to correct your practice when the teacher comes. You will have something you can ask about. Always in practice there are doubts and unclear places, which need clarification. If you don't do practice at all, if you're not familiar with the practice, and you get no results, then you have nothing to ask about, nothing to clarify. There's no sense in that, no meaning.

Generating kindness for others is easier when we remember that we had a connection with them as a mother and child, and when we remember their kindness, love, and care. When we remember their kindness and our relationship with them, then we begin to follow the process of allowing the kindness and care for them to flow. We don't have much problem to love and care for our husband or wife, our children, our parents, but we have problem to love, care and be kind to everyone in the society. It's difficult, right? Therefore, it's always good to generate kindness by remembering the kindness and love we have received from others, so that we have good reasons to be kind to them. Kindness towards them means taking care of them, solving their problems, and understanding their suffering. Kindness to others gives us more energy. It gives us greater possibility and reason to generate compassion.

## Nying Je: Compassion

Compassion comes after understanding that we are equal, appreciating the happiness and joy of others, and being kind to them. Then, we can be compassionate to their suffering in this khorwa, this cyclic existence. We can wish to overcome this suffering and liberate all the beings that once were our mothers and children from this suffering of existence.

It's not about having partial compassion. Even animals like tigers and snakes, the most harmful and violent beings, have partial compassion for themselves, for their children and close ones. We are talking about the compassion that is non-partial, boundless, without any limits, completely open for all sentient beings, like that generated by masters who achieved the state of Sanggye Tonpa Shenrab and the great masters from the past.

These four practices of equanimity, joy, kindness and compassion are the base for generating the mind of enlightenment. Compassion gives us strength, power, and energy to care and work for others, the attitude of willingness to care and solve the problems of others. Many times, the great masters, who generated real compassion from inside, cried for no apparent reason. Normal people looking at them thought them crazy, because there were crying, though there was no one in front of them. But they were crying, because they understood what real suffering means. Generally, in Bön, we say that this existing world is suffering.

I remember one story I heard in India in 1984, that happened during the Chinese Cultural Revolution. In the eastern part from Amdo, the region where His Holiness comes from, there was one lady named Ashi Khadro. *Ashi* means "respected, beloved." *Khadro* is a Tibetan word for *dakini* (Sanskrit). Ashi Khadro looked like an ordinary housewife. She was from a rich family. During the Cultural Revolution, her parents chose her a husband and she was married. But she didn't want to get married.

One day she disappeared from the village. Nobody knew what happened to her. People thought that she was dead. After many years they found that she was alive. She was found in complete solitude, in the forest. When Tibet was free she had received teachings on preliminary and actual practice. In the forest she had nothing to eat, she was there all by herself, and she had only one set of clothes. When people met her, she wasn't eating any food. She had great wisdom, she could tell the future, past, and even what you are thinking right now. If you were lucky, she would tell you about it, but she didn't always tell the future to everyone. Since the time she left, she had never entered a house or cave. You know the temperature and climate in Tibet, especially in winter, is very harsh. There is no way to survive outdoors unless you know some special practices. When Tibet regained some of its autonomy in '86, she returned to the village, because people were asking her to, but she always stayed outdoors.

People asked her how she survived. She said that all she ate was grass growing in the muddy areas. She survived by eating only this grass, with a bit of mud and some muddy water, and her practice. Everywhere this grass grows, there are also big horseflies. She said she mainly developed her patience, tolerance, and generosity because when she was meditating, the flies came and bit her. She said it was very painful at the beginning, but she remembered the practice of tolerance and patience, and she allowed them to bite her. After some time, she got used to it, and it was nothing for her. Afterward, lots of flies might come and drink her blood. She was doing the *tsa lung* practices, the practices of wind and channels, and also *tummo*. Even when it was raining she didn't get wet. It's not only her words, but people who saw her after 1986, when she started coming to the village, confirmed that. That time she sometimes took some milk, and it was considered great luck and a blessing if she accepted milk from some family.

One day a nomad family invited her in, because it was very cold, but she refused, saying that since the time she first left her village she never came under a roof. She stayed all night outside. During that night, a heavy snow fell, so people thought that she must have died, since it was very cold and she didn't have enough clothes. She only had her dress, worn out through so many years, almost gone, withered by wind and sun. Early in the morning, the housewife hurried out to see what happened to Ashi Khadro. She was perfectly fine; her clothes didn't even get wet. She was talking with people, prophesying, and sometimes, suddenly, she would burst into tears and say "Oh, I have to go. You don't see how sentient beings are suffering, I have to go, people are suffering, I have no time." Because of her wisdom, she saw the true suffering of people. And because of her experience of the four measureless practice, when she saw the nature of khorwa she generated real compassion to liberate beings from this suffering. So her tears came without planning, without expectations, from the power of her real insight.

The *bodhisattvas* (in Bön we call them *yungdrung sempa*, meaning *swastika-minded*) act this way. Moment after moment, they care for beings like that. If you really develop compassion like that, you will have inner feelings that will naturally occur, and you will care for others equally, without boundaries, without partialities. You will consider others more important than yourself.

When I heard that story I was very touched, and I very much wanted to meet her, to receive blessings, to have contact with her, exchange one or two words. I asked the person who told me about her to send me her photo. Some months later, when he went to

Tibet, he sent me her photo. By that time her behavior in the eyes of ordinary people seemed ugly. In the photo I received, she was really ugly. If I had seen that photo before I heard her story, I probably would not have understood it. In the photo she was wearing very ugly clothes, lying down on the road with a begging bowl. People considered her to be a crazy beggar.

In 1987 I decided to go to Tibet for the first time, to my monastery, Latri Monastery, in Kham. I especially wanted to go to the area where Ashi Khadro lived. It wasn't on our route, but still I decided to go there. I went there with one friend from our monastery, who is a lama and a tulku; and with a guide, the man who sent me the photo, who comes from Amdo. He accompanied me, although he didn't trust her. My friend, when he saw how she looked, wasn't ready to believe or trust her or be devoted to her. But I had no doubts. When I was in the guesthouse I saw her on the street, and I went out and tried to talk with her. I took a *katak* (scarf) in my hands to offer it to her. My guide introduced me to her. He very politely said, "Ashi Khadro, he has come from India and would like to talk with you and receive your blessing."

She was standing in front of a restaurant. I offered her the scarf. Because my guide was more familiar with Ashi Khadro, I asked my guide to ask her if she wanted something to eat. She got very angry and said a lot of things to my guide, which I didn't understand, because she was speaking very fast. She was very mad, I thought that she would hit me, but I understood her purely as a manifestation of a khadro, no matter how she was dressed. Her form wasn't important for me. All of a sudden, she took off all her clothes. In

Tibet we don't wear any underwear, and so she showed me her naked body, pointing to her vagina and saying, "Do you want to see this?" My guide was very afraid, and he ran away. But for me it was like showing me a secret mandala.

In ngag, we believe that a khadro's vagina is a secret mandala. I felt like she was removing all obstacles and showing me the mandala directly, granting me direct blessings. Her way of giving the blessing seemed, in the ordinary view, to be ugly, but in the ngag perception, it was a direct blessing. My friends thought I was foolish. They believed she was awful because of her outer appearance, and they thought I had too much blind faith. In my view, I saw the inner khadro who had given me a great blessing.

The point is, through compassion, we can feel the suffering of others, and comfort them as much as we can based on the level of our practice. We can dedicate ourselves to remove the suffering of others. Even if we are only sitting and thinking of others with real compassion, it's a great healing for them. The *yundrung sempas* (*bodhisatvas*) sometimes cried. They saw the suffering of other beings, were filled with compassion, and were spontaneously moved to tears.

## Three Levels of the Mind of Enlightenment

We have been discussing generating the mind of enlightenment. As we have said earlier, its main cause is the willingness to care for others, which comes mainly from compassion. There are three different levels of the mind of enlightenment, depending on the capacity of the practitioner. They can be seen as a shepherd; a guide; and a boatman.

The first way, the way of highest capacity, is *nag zi*, the way of the shepherd. The shepherd always sends his sheep before him, and he follows them. Like a shepherd, we may generate the wish for all sentient beings to achieve enlightenment first, and then for ourselves to achieve enlightenment next. We practice to attain enlightenment; but our goal is that others attain enlightenment and become free from suffering first.

The second way, the way of medium capacity, is *dru pa*, the way of the boatman. The boatman carries people in his boat. He steers the boat to the other shore, and both he and the people in his boat will get to the shore at the same time. In this way, we generate the wish that we may be liberated together with all sentient beings.

The third way, the way of lower capacity, is *lam khen*, the way of the guide. The guide has to know the place he is going and the way to get there. He needs to first have the knowledge and experience of the place he is guiding to first. He goes first and then comes back to show the way to the people he is guiding. In this way, we generate the wish to achieve enlightenment for ourselves first; only after achieving our own enlightenment will we go back to guide others to achieve enlightenment.

We can say that there is semkyed, the mind of compassion, that says, "may all sentient beings be free from suffering." To achieve this, we begin with *mon pa semkyed*, the inspirational wish or thought of the mind of enlightenment, which is the relative mind of enlightenment. *Mon pa semkyed* is our wish or prayer that all sentient beings are free from suffering. This is good, but it is incomplete if we don't act on it.

*Jug pa semkyed* is the thought or the determination to take action based on the *mon pa semkyed*. When we have strong compassion, we first wish that others may be free from suffering, and then decide we should put our wishes and prayers into action. When we have realized *jug pa semkyed*, we engage in practice to achieve this goal, such as practicing the *phar chin chu* (the ten transcendental perfections). We may contemplate the natural state of mind, recite *nyenpa* (Sanskrit *mantras*), or do any other virtuous actions. We take action by practicing, training ourselves, praying with the motivation to bring liberation to all sentient beings, and dedicating our merit for the benefit of others.

In this way, we see that the mind of enlightenment and compassion are two aspects of one face. When we practice compassion for other sentient beings, and when we develop the mind of enlightenment, the goal of both of them is to achieve enlightenment, with the understanding of suffering of beings in khorwa. First, we realize that we are equal with others, that others are equally important and deserve care. Next, we generate the attitude that others are more important than we are. In the third step, always, without any doubt or hesitation, we can take the place of others. If needed, in order to save others, to help and benefit them, we can sacrifice ourselves. This result comes mainly from practicing *mon pa semkyed*. Because of the power of this practice and its result, in early times, many masters adopted it as their main practice.

The semkyed practice is part of the preliminary practice, but it is not only "preliminary." You need to continuously base your practice on generating the mind of enlightenment and compassion until you achieve enlightenment.

One of great masters of Bön was Tulku Guru Nontse, a well-known *terton* (discoverer of hidden texts) and master of Dzogchen. Once, he was travelling and saw along the way, a very sick person in great pain with a bad toothache. He took this person's suffering on himself and felt the toothache for several days. That's how we care for others and take their pain, to release them from their suffering.

Guru Nontse didn't look like a lama and master. He looked like a great hunter, and he had his hunting dogs and weapons always with him. He spent time in the forest hunting, and it looked like he was killing wild animals, but actually he was liberating those beings from the form of a wild animal. Once there were several hunters, who weren't successful in killing any animals, and so they were suffering from hunger. Guru Nontse knew that they had been hunting for days without any result, so he manifested as a tiger and killed a deer, so they had some meat. Then he came back to human form and joined them. They shared the meat and talked, but some deer skin was stuck between his teeth. One of the hunters began to suspect him, that he might have transformed himself and killed the deer. After they finished eating, Guru Nontse collected the bones and wrapped them in the deer's skin, snapped his fingers, and the sack of bones transformed into a deer that stood up and ran away.

Guru Nontse's main purpose was to liberate sentient beings, to create a connection, in a good or a bad way, positive or negative, because all who had connection with him would be liberated. That was a purpose of his manifestation as a human being. He has never died. He made a statue of himself. He would ask people, "Who looks like this?" One day a man going on pilgrimage told him that the statue looked exactly like him, even with his dogs. Then Guru Nontse dissolved himself into the statue and remained as that statue. The statue lasted until the Cultural Revolution of 1959. It's beyond our ordinary thoughts and abilities, that's why it's a miracle, a manifestation.

This ability is rare. Only great spiritual masters manifested only to benefit sentient beings can do this. Often, we are not able to judge them by the way they look. Their inner wisdom, qualities and powers are not visible to our limited eyes. This story is just an example. There are many such stories in the teachings about performing such deeds. There are lamas who can actually perform these miracles. In order to see such miracles, we need a special eye, which is opened by trust and faith toward the lama, with complete inner respect.

During the Cultural Revolution, there was a lama who came from the famous lineage, Komtsang. His full name was Komtsang Lama Gyaltsen Norbu, but he was known as Uncle Lama. He lived in the area near Lhasa. He wore a Chinese hat and army cloak, used to laugh a lot, and never was serious. He was a high lineage lama. The Chinese tortured him, but he didn't care. He was tortured during the day. During the night, if somebody died, he went to that person's body and did phowa for him. The next day he was tortured again. He didn't care about himself, only about others. Even in those times, when everybody kept religious activities secret, he cared for the dying, carried them to the cemetery, and did the phowa for them. He was taking care for all this himself.

He was tortured by ordinary, common people, who asked him, "Where is your deity? Where is your power? Where are the three jewels?" These are not visible things that you can show to others.

Once, in 1986, a Tibetan communist died, a man who had tortured Uncle Lama a lot during the Cultural Revolution. His parents and wife were Buddhist, and they were very religious. The widow and son requested Uncle Lama to do phowa for the dead communist. He agreed. He told them to bring the body to the cemetery at a certain time, and to bring their relatives. Because the dead man was an important officer, many other officers and communists came. Uncle Lama said the prayers, covered his head, and did phowa for him. Everybody saw at the head of the dead man an eagle with a beard, and the eagle's upper neck was all in rainbow. All the people gathered at this ceremony saw this. When Uncle Lama had finished his practice, he asked the gathered people if they saw any signs. They explained what they had seen, and he replied to them, "That's good, you had at least seen the eagle, but in fact the man was liberated by Nyammed Sherab Gyaltsen, and you don't have to worry about him anymore."

These examples show that certain actions and powers don't depend on how we look or the way we act. Inner wisdom appears beyond boundaries and limits. It comes when the time is right, when there is a perfect capacity of those who see it to get blessing from it. All these powers come from practice. These masters have practiced and achieved powers. When we practice, from every practice comes a certain level of transformation, blessing, energy, and power. Practice transforms us and connects us with it. If we are not in the right position, then there is no way we can receive it.

These examples show us the results that may come from *mon pa semkyed* and *jug pa semkyed*, the two main types of generating the mind of enlightenment, the wish and action. Their result is arising equanimity, respect for others, and the ability to change ourselves for others, to care for others more than for ourselves. This all comes gradually according to our level of practice and understanding.

## A Practice to Generate the Mind of Enlightenment

To generate the mind of enlightenment, sit in the five-point posture. Understanding and thinking about everything that we have discussed so far, realize that all sentient beings have been our mothers and children. See their suffering. Feel that they don't understand the source of their suffering, and don't know how to overcome it. Think to yourself, "I am the one who has the knowledge of suffering, of the source of suffering, and of the way to overcome the suffering. That's why I should practice to generate the mind of enlightenment in this session, in this moment, to achieve the blessings and powers of enlightenment."

Continue, thinking, "All sentient beings are connected with me, as my mother and my children. They all are suffering in khorwa. They don't want or like khorwa, its conditions and suffering, but because of their ignorance, they are still cultivating the causes of suffering and experiencing the resulting negativities. Therefore I, being the child of all these sentient beings who were my mothers, am responsible to care for them and liberate them. But at this moment, I'm equally suffering, and I have no power, energy or blessings to liberate them. For this reason, I practice the semkyed, the mind of enlightenment. I ask my root teacher and the Sanggye of the ten directions to bless me and protect me."

We have to raise this thought in our heart, from deep inside us, and wish to achieve enlightenment so that every action of our body, speech, and mind would be useful and be part of liberating sentient beings. Recite the semkyed prayer and contemplate this state.

## Semkyed Prayer

*Ji tar gyal wa phag pa ji shin du*

*Di sog du sum ge we thu pal gyi*

*Sem chen sang gye thop par ja we chir*

*Dag ni jang chup chog tu semkyed do*


*As the Enlightened Ones and phagpas did,*

*By the power of the good virtues I have accumulated during the three times,*

*In order to bring all sentient beings to enlightenment,*

*I generate the mind of enlightenment.*

## The Merit Field: Kyab Dro Tsog Zhing

For the next practices of A-tri ngondro, we need to visualize what is called the *Kyab Dro Tsog Zhing*, the Merit Field, or sometimes the Refuge Tree. The A-tri text tells us to visualize Shenlha Ökar in front of us, above our crown. He sits on a throne held by snow lions, elephants, horses, dragons, and garudas, lifted up in the clouds. On the throne there are sun and moon cushions, and our root teacher sits on them. The text says he is in the form of Shenlha Ökar, but if you are familiar with Tapihritsa, you can visualize him. The deity is only the form that you visualize. But in reality, you are visualizing your root teacher in the form of a deity. According to this text, we visualize him as Shenlha Ökar. He has one face, two hands in equipoise position, and a white body. He is adorned with the thirteen peaceful ornaments. He is bright and full of light, liberating sentient beings by his kindness and compassion. You can also think that all the teachers with whom you are connected, even the person who taught you reading and writing, which is the seed and beginning of your spiritual practice, including all the teachers from whom you have received teachings, transmissions, and empowerments, are transformed into Shenlha Ökar.

His body is the Sanggye. His speech is Bön. His mind is pure, complete enlightened wisdom. Tsewang Rigdzin said that doing the lamé naljor practice and visualizing Shenlha Ökar as our teacher, is equal to visualizing the complete set of the tree of refuge and the Three Jewels. His body is an enlightened form, all his speech is teachings, and his mind is inseparable from Sanggye's mind, therefore the Three Jewels are present in him. And we transform our lama, our teacher, into the form of Shenlha Ökar. In this way he represents the Four Supreme Objects of Refuge, which are the Three Jewels and our lama.

Shenlha Ökar is surrounded by the chief yidam deities of Bön, such as Zhang Zhung Meri, Phurba, Takla, Sangdak, the Sanggye of the ten directions, and the khadros, protectors and lamas, who are lineage holders of these teachings. Above Shenlha Ökar, we see all the lineage holders of dho, ngag, and Dzogchen, the nine lineage holders of Dzogchen, holders of Dru, Shu, Pa and Me lineages, discoverers, translators, and others. These masters form lines leading up from Shenlha Ökar all the way back to Kuntu Zangpo, the Primordial Sanggye or Bönku. From the Bönku Kuntu Zangpo all the way to our teacher, we should see every master clearly, as bright and shining. Behind Shenlha Ökar there are representations of body, speech and mind of the Sanggye. Statues symbolize the body; texts symbolize speech; and stupas symbolize the mind of the Sanggye. Below him are all the male and female protectors, who expel all negativities and obstacles.

Nectar, flowing like water, comes from the heart of Kuntu Zangpo, the Primordial Sanggye. His body is blue, and he sits above the Merit Field. This nectar flows to all the masters and Sanggye who are below him, from one to another, and gradually flows to our teacher in the form of Shenlha Ökar, who is above our crown wheel. From Shenlha Ökar's heart it flows to our crown wheel. When the nectar from Shenlha Ökar's heart is transmitted to our crown wheel, at the same time it flows to all sentient beings and fills them.

It washes away all our negativities, obstacles and defilements. Our body is transformed into light, absolutely pure and clear. All the world and the objects surrounding us are transformed into light. Think that, in this way, we have received the full protection and blessing of the Three Jewels and Four Supreme Objects of Refuge, and are under their protection. When we visualize this process and feel that we have received protection from suffering, we are also protected from all the outer, inner and secret obstacles.

When we do these practices, we should have a clear picture of Shenlha Ökar, keeping in mind his color, position, ornaments and other details. If we are not able to visualize all those deities and khadros, it's fine. At the beginning we may start with seeing just Shenlha Ökar and clearly feeling his presence.

Do not just visualize the image of Shenlha Ökar and the others. Rather, try also to feel their real presence and essence. Otherwise, we will not get deep into the practice.

When we have finished the practice, we remain for a while in contemplation of the Merit Field without thought. Then, gradually, we dissolve everything as we have manifested it. We dissolve the whole Merit Field, beginning at the outside edges of the image and gradually moving to the center. Gradually, everything dissolves into light, and all light dissolves into the central figure of Shenlha Ökar. Then, Shenlha Ökar and his throne dissolve into light. This light flows to all sentient beings, including us. By dissolving the image, we have visualized into the light of wisdom, and we are unifying ourselves with the wisdom of our teachers and the Sanggye. We should feel that we have received all the blessings and qualities of body, speech, mind, wisdom, and action. Then, we dedicate the merit of that practice.

## Dedication

We should always dedicate our practice, even if we have only chanted a prayer once, or recited one *trengwa* (prayer beads; Sanskrit *mala*) of a prayer. Dedication is very powerful, and it brings great benefit. Our spiritual practice brings benefit to other beings only when we dedicate it.

Dedication develops our inner wisdom. It doesn't decrease the power of the practice. Dedication comes from our inside, and it changes our inner capacity. We learn to be more open and flexible.

Dedication has two purposes. It allows other beings to benefit from our practice. It also secures the merit of our practice from being destroyed by the actions of the five poisons (attachment, aversion, ignorance, pride, jealousy). We dedicate by a simple prayer, but there are many ways to dedicate merit. These ways differ in what, to whom, and how to dedicate. If we put a full meal on the table and do not invite guests or beggars from outside to eat it, then this food will not help to satisfy hunger. When we dedicate, our practice benefits the person to whom we dedicate. We can relate to this example and understand how the dedication works. In the case of beings that we don't see with our ordinary eyes, we can benefit them by dedication, by mental offering, by saying that it's for them, that they can have it. Only then they can benefit, because they are more connected with the mental aspect—they communicate mentally. Dedication is giving and protecting. Remember to dedicate every practice.

KYAB DRO TSOG ZHING – THE MERIT FIELD

# Kyabdro – Taking Refuge

The next part of the ngondro is the practice of taking refuge (kyabdro). *Kyab* means *protection*, and *dro* means *to go*. *Kyabdro* means going to someone for protection. We go for protection to the Three Jewels. The Three Jewels are: (1) Tonpa Shenrab, the enlightened one, Sanggye; (2) Bön, the teachings; and (3) Shenrab, the enlightened ones who have developed semkyed or bodhicitta. In Sanskrit these enlightened ones are called bodhisattvas, in Tibetan we call them *shenrab yungdrung sempa*. Westerners are more familiar with the Sanskrit names for the Three Jewels, which are Buddha, Dharma, and Sangha. We take refuge in these Three Jewels.

The A-tri text says that we take refuge in the Four Supreme Objects. In the Buddhist tradition, we talk about Three Jewels being the Sanggye, the teachings, and the bodhisattvas. In the Bön way, we also talk about the Three Jewels. But we also add the lama, our teacher. We add the lama because the lama is the one who is here with you, in a physical body, giving you the teachings and showing you the example of compassion. These are the Four Supreme Objects of Refuge. This is the best, most secure way of taking refuge and receiving protection.

Why do we take refuge? The refuge practice itself is called kyabdro, seeking protection. What kind of protection are we looking for? We ask the Three Jewels for protection, because we see the suffering, dangers, and fears of khorwa. We realize that we don't have the ability to overcome them, so we ask for protection from those beings who have the ability, power, and energy to protect us from this suffering and liberate us. If we didn't see the suffering and misery, then there would be no reason to seek refuge.

Taking refuge arises on the basis of trust. Trust means we believe without any doubt. There are four different types of trust.

## Trust of Inspiration

The first is the trust that arises because of inspiration, *moe pi tadpa*, the trust that arises because we are inspired by something we like. Its example is a child inspired by the mother it loves, who follows her without any fear or doubt. We may similarly develop faith coming from inspiration. When we go to temple, when we see a holy person, or great teachers, practitioners, simple monks, or when we go for pilgrimage, these kinds of things inspire us to follow their path, to practice, to follow the teachings, to work toward achieving enlightenment and liberating sentient beings. These feeling arise when we are inspired by some people and conditions. That kind of attitude is called trust from inspiration.

## Trust of Clarity

The second is *dang we tadpa*, trust from clarity. There is a special precious jewel, which when we put it into muddy water, clears it. Clarity of water appears when we put that jewel into water. That means that when we clearly understand suffering and its sources, and the enlightenment and power of the enlightened ones. We clearly see what to ignore and what to achieve.

## Trust of Belief

The third is *yi che pe tadpa*, the trust of belief that comes from realizing that khorwa is the result of negativities that we have committed in the past, that we experience now, and seeing that the qualities of the enlightenment and positive effects of the ten virtuous deeds come as a result of the practice. From this understanding without doubt of two different results, khorwa full of suffering, and enlightenment, joyful and positive, comes a decision to engage in practice, without any doubt or hesitation, and to achieve enlightenment. This is trust coming from clear understanding.

## Trust of Completion

The fourth is *thar chin pe tadpa*, the trust of completion. Our trust is completely unchanging, because we have a full understanding of the results of our actions. We renounce all the non-virtuous activities of body, mind, and speech. We completely engage in practice, knowing for certain, that we will not experience the results of negativities, because we practice virtuous deeds. Like a dead person, we have no doubt or hope. Once a man has died, he won't stand up again. In the same way, once we completely decide to involve ourselves in virtuous deeds and spiritual practice, then we will experience only the positive results and no suffering.

The practice of refuge is based on our trust and faith in the Three Jewels and the Four Supreme Objects of Refuge. If our faith is without doubt and without fear, it will open all the doors of the

Bön teachings. It will give us energy to enthusiastically follow the teachings. It will serve as the glue by which we can hold the teachings and understand them. The texts say that trust and faith open the door to Bön. Bön is the source of wisdom, of the teachings and practices that we receive. If we don't have trust in Bön, then we cannot receive its blessings and powers. The depth of our trust determines how much we will receive the fruit of blessings, wisdom, and experience. Therefore, it's better to practice with trust. If you have trust and faith, you will get results.

While you trust in Bön, be careful to avoid the wrong view towards other religions or sects, whether Buddhist, Hindu, Christian, or other. Each religion has its own essence, blessings, and methods to benefit, liberate, and help beings. In their essence, all religions aim to bring positive results, and not to harm others or cause negativities.

There is a true story from the early days about a mother and son. The mother was old and very devoted to Buddhist practice— especially to Buddha Shakyamuni. Her son went to India every year for business. She always asked him to bring her some auspicious religious objects, so she can pray and make offerings. She wanted something from India, the land of arhats, blessed by Buddha Shakyamuni. The son always answered that he would bring something, but he always forgot.

One time she warned him, that if this time he did not bring her some spiritual object from India to which she could be devoted, she would commit suicide in front of him the moment he walked through the door. He assured her, that this time he would definitely bring something. But again, in India he was very busy and completely forgot. He remembered about it only when he saw his house, but it was too late. He was worried, because his mother was very serious when she warned him that she would commit suicide. He thought that she might actually kill herself. So he thought he should have something with him to give her.

He looked around and he found a dog skeleton. He picked up one of the dog's teeth and wrapped it many times in a very expensive cloth, like a very auspicious item, and put it in his bag. When he came home, his mother offered him tea, and asked him if he remembered her request. He said that of course he remembered, and had brought her very precious gift that was very hard to obtain. And he took it out of his bag, unwrapped the cloth, and told her it was a tooth of Buddha Shakyamuni. She was so delighted, touched and happy. She put it on her altar and prayed every day, offering incense, water, lamps. She cleaned it and did prostrations. She was happy and fulfilled.

One day, when mother wasn't there, the son peeked into her room to see what happed to the tooth. The tooth had many *ringsel* (bits of new bone that grow out of the bone or tooth of an enlightened being, as a blessing) relics around it. He was surprised, because he knew that this was a dog's tooth, but still it produced *ringsel*. That is the power of doubtless, fearless faith. If you decide with complete devotion that the tooth is a tooth of Buddha, then even if it has the form of a dog's tooth, in your perception it will be Buddha Shakyamuni's tooth. The power of your pure trust produces results, like the *ringsel* that appeared on the tooth. It appeared because of the blessing of Buddha Shakyamuni, who said that whoever trusts and practices according to his words will experience results. The teachings of the Sanggye have no tricks. Each and every word is completely true and pure. We should have the same trust as the woman in this example. We should have faith in the Three Jewels in order to protect us from the suffering of this world, of the miserable conditions we experience every day.

I say, "miserable conditions, endless suffering," although I don't know how you view it. Once, I had a discussion with several students. One person told me that he enjoys this life. He thinks it's a gift of God, and he was afraid of *nyangde* (enlightenment; Sanskrit nirvana), because he thought that once he achieved enlightenment, he would lose joy in his life. He had no trust in enlightenment, in the qualities and powers of the Sanggye. He had no deeper understanding of the reality of khorwa, how we are circulating in it because of the influence of the five poisons, and how it gives birth to suffering. He didn't understand that. The power, blessing, and energy of enlightenment is not something visible, but it depends on trust and belief.

The blessings of the Three Jewels are like a hook, thrown out to us on a cord. We need a ring, so the hook has something to hook onto. We practitioners have the ring of trust, and the Three Jewels have the hook of blessings. When they throw the hook of blessings, we need the ring of trust, so the hook can attach to the ring and we can receive their blessings. If you don't have a ring of trust that the hook can attach to, there's no way to receive the blessings. If we have both the ring and hook, then neither the distance nor our physical body matters. No matter where the spiritual realm is, thanks to our trust, we are connected with it, and we receive blessings and protection. This is how we are protected by the Three Jewels. To take refuge in Three Jewels, you must really trust them and have faith in them.

## A Refuge Practice

Sit cross-legged in the five-point meditation position. Put your hands together over your heart, as a symbol that you are taking full refuge. Bow, or sit in a contemplation posture. Generate the attitude of trust to the Three Jewels, with an understanding of suffering and why you are seeking protection. Relax, free yourself from pressure and abide in a state of contemplation.

Visualize the Merit Field as described earlier. Visualize Shenlha Ökar above your crown wheel, facing toward you. Visualize all the other elements of the Merit Field. Visualize all other sentient beings behind us. With a clear vision of all this, we imagine ourselves as leading all sentient beings. Visualize that not only are you taking refuge, but you are leading all the other sentient beings behind us in taking refuge. We lead them and prostrate to the Three Jewels and deities we have visualized. We generate the thought that, from today until we achieve enlightenment, we bow down with complete devotion to Shenlha Ökar and the deities surrounding him, asking for protection from the miserable conditions of khorwa, from the suffering of this world of existence.

Think of how all sentient beings are suffering in khorwa, and take refuge from suffering in the Three Jewels, requesting in your mind: "We, sentient beings, endlessly suffer from this miserable condition. You have the power to protect us. We trust only in you, and we rely on you. Please protect us. You are the only ones we can rely on. Only you have the wisdom, power, and compassion to lead all sentient beings to liberation. We are devoted to you." Think that you are leading all sentient beings, and you are doing prostrations and circumambulations of the Sanggye's forms, seeking blessings and protection.

Generate this thought from deep inside in a sharp, distinct way. The signs of doing this correctly are that all the hairs on our body stand on end, and tears spontaneously flow. It won't happen right away, but by practicing seriously, the results will come, and you will experience it. We are not only seeking protection from the suffering of khorwa, but we also seek guidance through the uncertainty and lack of clarity, impeding us from making the right decisions. We ask for protection from all obstacles that may appear in our three periods: this life, the bardo, and our next rebirth.

While you visualize Shenlha Ökar, see a shower of nectar coming from his heart, down to our crown wheel and to all sentient beings. When the nectar from Shenlha Ökar's heart is transmitted to our crown wheel, visualize that it flows to all sentient beings and fills them, washing away all negativities, obstacles, and defilements. Our body is transformed into light, absolutely pure and clear. All the world and the objects surrounding us are transformed into light. Think that, in this way, we have received the full protection and blessing and are under the protection of the Three Jewels and Four Supreme Objects of Refuge. When we visualize this process and feel that we have received protection from suffering, we are also protected from all the outer, inner, and secret obstacles. Then, recite the prayer of kyabdro:

## Kyabdro Prayer

*Shenrab, lama, ku sum jung ne pal,*

*Du sum der shek dro wa yong kyi gon,*

*Ku zug shal kyin ku dung sung rab ten,*

*Chok chu shenrab tar lam ton pe dron*

*Ne shir chak tsal dro kun kyap su chi.*


*Root lama, magnificent source of the three bodies,*

*Enlightened Ones of the three time, the principal savior of sentient beings,*

*The stupas and scriptures that represent the Enlightened Ones and their teachings,*

*Enlightened Ones of the ten directions, who are the lamps on the path of liberation,*

*We prostrate and take refuge in these four supreme objects of refuge.*

After completing the recitation, imagine that the Merit Field dissolves into Shenlha Ökar, who dissolves into light, and that we become unified with him. Try to remain in that state, with clarity and peace, and without thought.

## Confession

The third practice of the second session of ngondro is confession (*shagpa*). Tonpa Shenrab, the Enlightened One, gave many teachings. Among them are methods to purify the results of negative actions that we have performed in the past. He also told us what the virtuous and non-virtuous deeds are. He showed us the method to cultivate the virtuous deeds and positive results, and how to overcome negativities. One important way to do this is through confession.

Through the practice of confession, we decrease the energy of our negativities. If we take some grain, like rice, barley, or corn, and fry it, and then plant it, it will not grow, because we have taken the energy of growth. When we confess our negative deeds, from then on, the growth of their negative results will discontinue. But we have to apply the practice to clean and remove whatever we have cultivated in the past, so it doesn't continue to grow results. Most of what we experience in this cyclic world is caused by our negative karma. This cause may be near or distant, sooner or later, immediate or delayed. It may come from this life, or from some past life long ago. There are many gradual ways in which the results of negativities arise. Because we haven't purified causes from the past, we experience their results in this lifetime. We practice confession to purify them and discontinue their growth, so we may be free from their results in next lifetimes, or maybe even in this life.

We all think that we are good practitioners, meditating on emptiness, or the natural state of mind, or practicing with a deity. Whatever our practice, as long as we don't fully confess, our negativities keep growing. They will obstruct our development and create obstacles to our wisdom and achieving realization.

I don't know exactly what you think when I talk about negative deeds and actions and obstacles. It's not necessary to kill someone or break someone's leg. Every moment in our mind, thoughts arise. Some are positive, and others are negative. It's like a print we leave behind. When we step on the ground, our footprint stays even when we take away the foot. The power and energy of negative deeds similarly leave a print.

A mirror has the ability to reflect all the objects in the room it faces—or your face if you stand before it. But if it is covered by dust, it will show no reflection, even though it has the potential to reflect. It is the same way with our natural state of mind. The natural state of mind has clarity and reflects reality; but we will not be able to see it until we remove the dust that covers it. The print of our negative deeds blocks us from seeing our true nature.

There are two kinds of defilements: (i) defilements that will block us from achieving realization, and (ii) defilements preventing us from achieving enlightenment and omniscient wisdom. Both of them are blocking us. That's why it's important to practice and purify them.

# The Four Powers of Confession

When we practice confession, we should observe the four conditions, or four powers, of confession. These are: (i) the power of regret for our past wrong deeds; (ii) the power of commitment not to repeat them; (iii) the power of the antidote by practice; and (iv) the power of the witness in front of whom we confess.

If we do our practice of confession with a perfection of these four powers, we prevent the continuation of growth of negativities that we have cultivated in the past.

## The Power of Regret for Past Deeds

When we practice shagpa, we must think of all the negativities that we remember, and also those we don't remember, from all our past lives until now. This means all negative deeds done through body, speech and mind, directly and actively. It also means negative deeds we directly or indirectly inspired others to do, or appreciated when others did. Think, "All negativities, from the smallest to the largest, that I have done until now, intentionally and without knowing, I confess without hiding in front of the Sanggye, teachers and protectors. I regret these negative deeds and resolve not to do them again. I confess all these deeds to purify them."

If we regret all past deeds that we have cultivated, with or without intent, everything can be purified and cleansed. As long as we regret and remember what we have done, we may purify it. The text says, that if we regret very deeply from our heart, then any of the actions of body, speech, and mind we may have cultivated, no matter how serious and negative, can be purified. There are always methods to overcome them. While regretting our misdeeds, we have to commit that, from today on, we will engage in practice and keep away from all negativities, avoiding even the smallest non-virtuous deeds. We will also inspire others to practice, engage in virtuous deeds, and appreciate everyone who practices and performs them.

## The Power of Commitment Not To Repeat

When we have expressed all our negative deeds, it's not enough to just regret them. We have to commit that, from now on, we will not repeat such actions again. This is the power of commitment. But this is also not enough. Through our commitment, we stop negativities from growing, but we haven't removed them. To remove them, we need an antidote.

We have to apply our practice in this current time to purify and heal the negativities that we have cultivated in the past. Many sicknesses in our life and in our body are connected with our past actions, and we cannot heal or overcome them just by taking medicines.

## The Power of the Antidote

The best way to practice the antidote is to practice by ourselves, if our health allows. We can recite prayers of purification, depending on the practice that we have received. In most cases, when we receive the teachings on ngondro, we do the hundred-syllable recitation (*yig gya*). This recitation contains the collective seed syllables of the deities. By reciting it, we purify and clear our negative deeds. Through the dedication prayer, we dedicate the merit of our practice to all sentient beings, so they can benefit from our practice and virtuous deeds.

We can also ask lamas to perform practices and recite holy texts for us. We can do acts of generosity by giving food to homeless people, etc. We can sponsor monks to perform religious ceremonies, to recite prayers of long life or overcoming obstacles. We can also simply make a tea offering for monks.

### The Power of the Witness

What is the power of the witnesses? When we perform our confession and make our commitment not to repeat the non-virtuous deeds in the presence of a witness, our confession and commitment are much stronger. The witness can be a person; we can go to any lama and explain our negativities to him. Or the witness can be an image of a deity. We can go to a temple where there is a statue of Tonpa Shenrab, or an image of Chamma, the Loving Mother, or Shenlha Ökar. If we cannot go to a temple or find a statue or thangka, we can just visualize Shenlha Ökar in front of us, in a circle of rainbow, feel their presence above our crown wheel, and confess to them. Standing in front of them, we feel their presence. We should perceive them not just as a sculpture or painting, but we feel that they really are present in front of us.

With this strong feeling of presence, we confess our negative deeds with deep regret. We express all the negative deeds that we remember, and we also include all those we don't remember, with the intention of confessing and purifying all the negativities we may have committed from the beginning of time until now, during all our lives in this cyclic existence. We commit to not perform non-virtuous deeds in the presence of the witness, which makes our commitment stronger. This is the power of the witness.

## A Confession Practice

Sit in five-point posture in front of your shrine, a statue of the Sanggye or Shenrab, a painting, thangka, or image of your teacher. Or, visualize Shenlha Ökar, a protector like Yeshe Walmo, a deity like Meri, or another, in the space above your crown wheel. You can also visualize the Merit Field as described earlier.

Think of all the negative deeds you have done, from previous lives to this one. Generate a strong attitude of regret for these negative deeds from deep inside and confess these negative deeds.

Standing in front of the witness, whether Shenlha Ökar or other, we confess our misdeeds and request blessing. From their heart, they produce rays and lights that go to all sentient beings. When these rays and lights touch our crowns, they transform into liquid nectar, filling our body and bodies of all beings, and cleansing our bodies, so that all negativities drain out of our bodies through our lower organs and from under our toenails, and come out in the form of dirty, black liquid. From that liquid a dark blue smoke rises, representing all the negativities that are removed from you.

Then perform an antidote practice, such as reciting the one hundred syllable yig gya *nyenpa* (*mantra*):

# Yig Gya

*SO MU YE TRO KHYUNG YE LAM TRI TRI*
*TAR DAR*

*SAL BAR Ö PAG RAM SO HA*

*SO MU RA TA HEN WER NI DRUM RHUN*

*MU TE MU TE MU RA MU TE*

*MU YE MU YE HARA MU YE*

*MO TOE MO TOE WER RO MU TOE*

*MU NI GYER TOE YE KHYAB KHAR RO*

*TOE DAL RHI RHO WER NI WER RO*

*SHU LA WER RO NA HU TA KA*

*SHUD DO SHUD DO DU SHUD DO YA*

*SAL LE SAL LE TI SAL LE YA*

*SANG NGE SANG NGE SU SANG NGE YA*

*MU RA TO HAN TRI TSE DUNG MU*

*HA HA DRUM DRUM HO HO LAM LAM*
*HUNG HUNG*

*PHÄT PHÄT*

Then, dedicate your practice for the benefit of all sentient beings.

The text advises us to practice the confession practice at least for a week or nine days, as a retreat. Of course, we can practice it always in our daily life. After waking up in the morning we may pray to our root teacher, deity, or our protector, asking them for blessings, and asking them to protect us from doing non-virtuous deeds. At the end of the day, before going to bed, we may think about what we have done during this day, what were the virtuous deeds that we may be happy with, and what were the negative deeds, causing harm, injuring others, intentionally or unintentionally, and regret them and ask for purification. We can do it every day.

In early times in Tibet, we didn't have a system of surgery. The lamas would advise patients, even those who were very sick and could hardly stand and travel, to go on a pilgrimage to a holy mountain and do prostrations there. The lama would advise them to do 500 or 1000 prostrations or circumambulate the place three times. If a patient did this with full devotion, he received signs of his practice.

In Tibet there is a holy mountain of the Bön tradition, called Kongpo Bönri. The name Kongpo Bönri means "the holy mountain of Bön in the Kongpo valley." If you go to Tibet, you should visit this place. It's not far from Lhasa, about six hours by bus. There are also many caves there, where great practitioners lived.

Tonpa Shenrab gave his first teachings in Tibet in that valley, and he transferred his wisdom into the special rock in the center of that mountain, called Kunzang Thugkar, Heart of Kuntu Zangpo. This rock has a very special shape, and self-arising images of the liberators of the six realms (*dhulwa shen drug*) and the Three Heart Essences of Bön (*nyingpo nam sum*) appear on it. In the whole mountain, many self-arising images of Sanggye, *nyingpo*, and also *yungdrung* symbols, appear on the rock. In the four directions of that mountain are four rocks shaped like thrones, and on the side of these rocks are self-arising *nyenpa*. These are the thrones on which Tonpa Shenrab is said to have sat. I've been there three times and have seen the self-arising *nyingpo* on two of the rocks.

It's a wonderful, inspiring place. All year round there are hundreds of people, circumambulating the mountain, doing prostrations, circumambulating it by doing flat prostrations, and so on. In the Bönpo tradition, each family tries to go there at least once in a lifetime. If someone doesn't go there at least once, he feels he hasn't achieved anything. Most families try to go there every year or every other year, sending someone else each time: those who have to take care of animals would rather go in winter, and some businessman prefer to go in summer. Everybody is trying to go there. And many sick people are advised by their lamas that their sickness is caused by past actions, and therefor they should go to a holy place like this and do prostrations. After such practice, they often vomit their sickness out, or it goes away in other way. Not only Bönpos, but even Buddhists come to circumambulate that mountain. We believe some sicknesses may be cured only by spiritual practice and purification. Of course, some of the sicknesses can be healed by medicine, but for us it's important to practice purification by confession practice.

In our monastery, on the fifteenth day of every month, all monks wake up at 5:00 a.m., including His Holiness and Lopon Rinpoche. We all come to the temple to do the purification ritual called *so jong*. *So* means filling up whatever has decreased, filling up our wisdom and practices. *Jong* means purifying and clearing all negative deeds and minor transgressions against our discipline and practice. All this we recall and express in our mind in front of Sanggye Tonpa Shenrab's statue and ask His Holiness and other senior lamas to purify us. We do this every month. At the end of the prayer, His Holiness asks us if we remember our wrong deeds, and if we are committed not to do them again. We all answer "yes, yes," and at the end he tells us we have purified these negativities.

Individually, everybody should try to do this practice at the end of every day. We should reflect on our deeds of the day, both good and bad. For the wrong deeds, we should acknowledge them, do a cleansing prayer or action, and commit not to do them again. For the good or positive deeds, we should dedicate the merit to all sentient beings.

# Mandala Offering

The third part of the ngondro is the *mandala* offering. The purpose of this offering is to accumulate merit. There are two types of merit. The first is the Merit of Cause. The Merit of Cause is the accumulation of prosperity from all virtuous actions we perform, such as offerings, *tsok*, or others. The second is the Merit of Result. The Merit of Result is an internal growth of realization or wisdom that arises from the accumulation of prosperity; we become aware of the prosperity and derive wisdom from it. The Merit of Cause accumulates prosperity and fortune that allows us to practice and achieve realization. The Merit of Result is when we receive the understanding and the wisdom of realization because of the blessing and power of the Merit of Cause.

If either of these two is absent, then we will not obtain the perfect result from our practice, or we may face obstacles in our practice. Often, when people practice, they experience obstacles, such as sickness that doesn't allow them to continue their practice. We need to cultivate merit to overcome these obstacles.

There are many ways to cultivate merit. The A-tri ngondro text says that, among all the material offerings and virtuous deeds, offering the mandala is one of the most powerful and beneficial. Other texts also say the mandala offering is the best way to cultivate merit.

Always, when we do any practice, we start with the common prayers: *nyammed sol deb* (the one that begins with "*dechen gyalpo*"); kyabdro (taking refuge); semkyed (generating the mind of enlightenment); and lamé naljor (the practice of our root teacher, which deepens our devotion and obtains blessings for realization). Whenever we practice, we start with these prayers, because it's important to generate the right attitude of mind, to take refuge in the Three Jewels, to generate the proper intention, and to receive blessing and wisdom from our root teacher. Also, we perform a confession practice, remembering our negative deeds and purifying ourselves before we start the practice of cultivating merit.

When we perform the mandala offering, we should use the mandala plates made of gold, silver, or other precious metals if we can, or even plates made from wood or some other material. We use the foundation plate and three rings. We fill the rings with rice, barley, corn, jewels, turquoise, coral, coins, etc. mixed with grain, and then we put a top on that. This material mandala can be made of different materials, but it has to have perfect quality, with no defect. If the material has defects, this may also affect your luck and prosperity. The text says that if the mandala plates are made of gold or silver, then the base plate can have a diameter of three or four inches. If it's made of wood or other material, then it can be wider.

We start with cleansing the plates and reciting the nyenpa. Then, we put some grain in the center of the plate, then some grain in each of the four directions and four sub directions. Then, we gradually build the whole mandala up. Cleansing the mandala symbolizes cleansing past karma. It will make us healthier, prevent sicknesses, and help us to develop wisdom. This is what the text says.

When we cleanse the mandala, we hold it in our hands, and say:

*NAMO AKAR SHAYA NI SHAK SALE SANGE SO HA*

Then, we place the grain in the center, saying:

*DRUM RI TI GAR MA LA HO*

We place grain in the four directions and four sub-directions, saying:

*A YAM RAM MAM KHAM DRUM SHAK SALE SANGE SO HA*

We start with the side of mandala closest to us, which is considered to be east, and then we go anticlockwise, center and east, north, west, south. We fill the whole mandala with grain as we say:

*CHO PUR SA LE HA LO SENG*

When the foundation plate is filled, we put the first ring on it and fill it up, and then the second ring and the top. Then, holding the whole mandala, we offer it with the prayer. Normally, we use the prayer given below.

When building up the mandala, be careful to be very precise. Don't put more rice on one side and less on the other, because it also affects our practice, fortune, and realization of wisdom.

When we hold the mandala, we visualize the Merit Field. We need to build this vision clearly, bright like stars in the sky.

Then, we begin to prepare the mandala. When we have the mandala ready in our hand, we can multiply it and manifest it as a whole universe. Because it is only a symbol of the universe, we can offer the whole universe as a mandala. We do this by seeing the whole earth as if made of gold, with Mount Meru in the center, surrounded by seven great golden mountains and seven great lakes, surrounded by four great worlds in four directions, and eight continents, and all this world surrounded by an ocean. All the objects within this world are offerings, jewels, precious gems, gold, silver, all the minerals, and other precious things. We are leading all sentient beings; each of them carries this precious offering to the Sanggye. Prepare to offer it without attachment or greed, seeking blessing of wisdom and merit, to receive and observe high teachings.

As if we were standing in front of the Sanggye, we request: "We, sentient beings, offer you all these precious objects, and in return we ask you to grant us with achievement of realization and experience of understanding of the natural state of mind, here in this session, on this meditation cushion. Please also remove all the outer, inner, and secret obstacles we practitioners encounter, by the blessing of this mandala offering." Then, we offer it with the prayer. We can multiply the mandala in our vision, according to our ability to visualize. We receive blessings and ask the Sanggye to bless all sentient beings and their environment. And we repeat this process, preparing the mandala and offering it. After one hundred repetitions, we should change the rice or grain we use, so as not to use the same too many times; but we may use the same coins, turquoise, and other non-grain offerings.

At the end of our session, we shouldn't just pour the grain from the mandala plates. There is special way of removing it, from left to right, with a prayer. We shouldn't eat the grain afterwards, but generously give it to birds or other beings. Then, we dissolve our visualization, moving from the sides to the center. All the deities, khadros, protectors, and masters dissolve, one into another, and eventually they all dissolve into the central figure of Shenlha Ökar; then he dissolves into us. All the sentient beings and the whole universe and offering objects dissolve into the space of natural emptiness. Again, we ask for blessings and removal of all negativities. We should practice this way, doing as many repetitions as we can, for example, one hundred in the morning and one hundred in the evening, until we complete one hundred thousand repetitions of the mandala offering.

If we don't have material mandala plates, we can use hand gestures. First, we hold our palms together, left hand down with palm facing up and right hand up with palm facing down. We make a circle with the right hand, three times counterclockwise, to clean the past; then three times clockwise, to clean the present, and then three times forward, to clean the future. In this way we clean all the negativities, non-virtuous deeds, and karmas. When you do this, it's important to really think that you are cleansing these negativities.

After purifying the negativities of the three times, we make the gesture of building the mandala. With our hands we symbolically build Mount Meru, four worlds and eight continents, and then we offer it with a prayer. When we say words *"bül lo,"* we snap our fingers. Snapping our fingers signifies we have no attachment; we let it go. This way, we complete one hundred thousand repetitions.

## Mandal Bülwa

*É ma jung ngé teng du ri rab ri dün dang*

*Ling zhi ling tren chi nang dö yön ché*

*Nyi zhi gyen pa jewa trag gya di*

*Dag gi lö lang bül lo zhé su sol*


*On top of the five elements, Mount Meru, and the seven circling mountains,*

*Together with internal and external objects of enjoyment of the four continents and the subcontinents,*

*And countless universes decorated with sun and moon,*

*Please accept this offering from the core of my heart.*

Shenlha Ökar – Enlightened One of Compassion

# Lamé Naljor

Now comes the fourth and last part of the ngondro, the practice of *lamé naljor* (connecting to the teacher; Sanskrit *guru yoga*). This is a practice of prostration to the great masters, to invoke them and receive their blessing.

In the past, this practice was included in the same chapter with kyabdro (taking refuge) and semkyed (generating the mind of enlightenment). There was no separate session of this practice. But Dogon Lodo Gyaltsen, the teacher of Nyammed Sherab Gyaltsen, said it was important to have a separate session of the lamé naljor practice. He said that although the butter comes from milk, until you churn the milk, you won't get butter. Iron is contained in iron ore, but until you melt it, you won't get iron. The blessing, energy, quality, and power of the teacher and the Three Jewels is the source of blessings, but you will not receive them until you pray with devotion and connect to the Sanggye. So we, especially beginners, should engage in the practice of trust, faith, inspiration, and prayer to the teachers and Sanggye. The result and development of our practice, the blessing and inspiration we receive, and the development of our inner wisdom all depend on the blessing and powers of the Three Jewels. Therefore, it's important to practice with trust, faith, and inspiration. That is why we need a separate session of this practice.

To practice lamé naljor, we sit in the five-point meditation position. We visualize the Merit Field and visualize our teacher in the form of Shenlha Ökar above our crown wheel, on his throne. Visualize all the elements of the Merit Field.

Visualize that we sit below all these deities and in front of all sentient beings including our enemies and people we don't like. Visualize that we are not alone, that we lead all sentient beings to the deities, as we prostrate and wish that all sentient beings, those who are unfortunate, haven't cultivated enough merit, and are suffering in cyclic existence, be protected and guided to overcome suffering. We ask the deities of the Merit Field to purify all our negativities and karmic traces, because we trust and believe in them, and because they have the power, ability, and blessing to protect and liberate us. We have to raise this thought from deep inside, we need to awaken ourselves by understanding the practice, with complete devotion, trust, and surrender to them.

Visualize that wisdom, in the form of nectar, flows from Bönku Kuntu Zangpo, through all the masters and to Shenlha Ökar.

Visualize that the nectar flows from Shenlha Ökar's heart to our crown wheel, and at the same time it flows to all sentient beings. This nectar fills us all up, washing away all negativities, obstacles, and defilements. Our body is transformed into a body of light, absolutely pure and clear. All the world and objects surrounding us are transformed into light. We must feel that we are clean and purified.

Then we ask for the blessing and power of the actions of the enlightened ones, by which we can also serve others, help them, guide and liberate them. We ask the Sanggye to grant us the five qualities of enlightenment, in this session of our practice, in this moment, on this cushion. We ask for blessing, protection, and the five qualities of enlightenment. Then, with the intention and visualization that we have mentioned earlier, with complete inner devotion, we recite the recitation prayer of lamé naljor:

## Lamé Naljor Prayer

*Chi tsug de wa chen po pho drang du*

*Drin chen tsa we la ma la sol wa deb*

*Sanggye sem su ton pa Rinpoche*

*Rang ngo rang gi she par jin gyi lob*


*In the palace of great bliss above my crown,*

*I pray to you, benevolent Root Lama,*

*The Precious One who reveals the enlightened nature of my mind.*

*Bless me that I may recognize it as my own nature of mind.*

When we conclude this practice, dissolve all sentient beings, in the form of rays and light, into the space where you have visualized the Enlightened Ones. Then, dissolve all of those visions into the central figure of Shenlha Ökar, which then dissolves into light that flows into you. Think that you have received the quality of the absolute mind of enlightenment and meditate on this without the distraction of thoughts. By doing this, we are unifying ourselves with the wisdom of our teachers and the Enlightened Ones. We should feel that we have received all the blessings and qualities of body, speech, mind, wisdom and action. Then, we should dedicate the merit of that practice.

## The Right View of the Teacher

The teachings stress that we have to learn the right way to follow the teacher. Whether the student respects the teacher or not doesn't make any difference to the teacher; but it does make a difference for the student, because it changes the way he receives the teachings and their benefit. The texts mention again and again, before any teachings, the student should take refuge, generate the mind of enlightenment, and pray to the lamas. Paying respect to the teacher doesn't change anything for the teacher, but changes everything for the practitioner.

Depending on the student's view of the lama, the student will receive a different level of benefit. The teachings say that if we view our lama as a real, present Sanggye, such as Shenlha Ökar, we will receive all his teachings as the nectar of blessings flowing to us. But if we view our lama as a businessman, then whatever we receive from him will only bring us benefit as if it were an object for trade. And if we view our lama as a dog, then whatever he teaches will bring us the same benefit as dog food.

In early times, there was a great lama who was a really great practitioner. But he didn't look like a lama or behave like one. He was famous, respected, and had great knowledge, but he didn't look like it. He looked like an ugly, simple lay person. Because of his fame, people came to him from all over eastern and upper Tibet. One man was very inspired by the stories he heard about this lama and decided to go visit him and receive teachings. To get to the lama, the man had to walk for six months. When he finally reached the village where the lama lived, he asked the people there where he could find the lama. The villagers told him the lama was probably working in the field. The man went to the field and saw that the lama was plowing the field, and his wife was planting it. He was shocked to see this, because normally practitioners don't plow fields, to avoid killing insects that live there. The man was very disappointed that the lama about whom he heard so may stories was doing such a sinful thing. The man thought all his effort to come visit the lama was wasted. But he decided that, since he had already come that far, he would go to the lama.

The lama saw the man and asked him who was he looking for. When the man answered that he was looking for the lama, the lama told him to go to his house and wait for him. The man wondered what he should do. Should he ask the lama for teachings? Should he leave? He was very uncertain. The lama came in the evening, and they shared a meal. The lama told him to stay the night in his house and promised him they would talk in the morning. The lama knew that the man had an incorrect view toward him, so the lama gave the man a chance to change his attitude.

In the morning, the lama asked the man to come to his shrine room. The man decided that he would not ask the lama for teachings, but would first ask him for an initiation, to see what the lama would give him and how he would feel. When the lama asked him what he wanted, the man asked for an initiation. Then, the lama opened his chest and showed the man a full set of wrathful and peaceful deities in his heart.

Then the lama asked him who he wanted to receive the initiation from: from the yidam deity, or from the lama. The man thought the yidam was much more special, so he asked for the initiation from the yidam. Then, the vision disappeared. The lama told the man to go away. He told the man that he was trying to transform his wrong view and gave him a chance, but the man still couldn't overcome his dualistic thoughts. The lama told the man to change his attitude first, and then come for teachings. So, the man received nothing. The deity the lama showed the man was inseparable from the lama himself; but the student couldn't understand that.

In this worldly life, we pay attention to material things, such as how famous someone is or how many assistants he has. These things make a difference to us. But inner wisdom does not depend on our fame or our looks. The more wisdom we have, the simpler we live. We shouldn't judge teachers by their looks. We should try to trust them and benefit from them. They are the source of our wisdom and understanding. All we have received now comes from our teacher. Often, there are practitioners who, after they have learned a little bit, try to ignore their teacher, to move away from him. Sometimes they cultivate negative views toward him. This is completely wrong. These practitioners are cultivating negative karma and blocking their development. As the texts say, whenever you practice, pray to your root teachers, to whom you are devoted, with whom you are connected, and seek their blessings.

The practice of lamé naljor is based on receiving blessings. We have to judge for ourselves whether we have received the blessings or not. If we feel that through the gradual process of practice, we have received the blessings, then yes, we have received them. And if we don't feel it, it means we haven't received them, and we have to practice more.

In a state of meditation, we should feel that we have not only purified ourselves, but also transformed our ordinary body, speech, and mind into the quality of the Sanggye and our teacher; that we are completely unified. Our physical, ordinary body, speech, and mind are no longer ordinary, because they have been transformed into the state of Shenlha Ökar. Therefore, when we have done the purification part of the practice, we have to feel that we are purified and ready to receive the wisdom, and to become inseparable from the Sanggye. It's possible, because we are ready for it; we have transformed our body into a crystal body, a body of light.

## The Five Qualities of Enlightenment

Through lamé naljor, we ask that the five qualities of enlightenment be transferred to us. The five qualities of enlightenment are:

| | |
|---|---|
| Body | (*A*) |
| Speech | (*OM*) |
| Mind | (*HUNG*) |
| Quality or Energy | (*RAM*) |
| Action | (*DZA*) |

We have discussed transforming our ordinary body, speech, and mind into the pure body, speech, and mind of the Sanggye.

We also wish that all our actions serve to guide and liberate all sentient beings. In Tibetan, this is called *dro don*. *Dro* is the short name for all sentient beings, *drowa semchen*. *Don* is purpose. *Dro don* means that we practice helping sentient beings, guide them, and liberate them.

Still that is not enough. We need a way to carry this responsibility. Taking care of other sentient beings is not a simple job. We know how difficult it is to care for our family, how much work it takes, how much we worry, how big a responsibility it is. When we talk about caring for all sentient beings, the way is the same, but the scope or capacity is broader. We not only want to care for them on the physical level, but we try to liberate them from khorwa, cyclic existence. For this, we need *thab*, which is method, energy, compassion. Only then will we be able to help other beings.

In lamé naljor practice, we ask the Sanggye to grant us these qualities, in this session of our practice, in this moment, on this cushion. We ask for blessing, protection, and the five qualities of enlightenment. With full awareness, we ask to receive all these blessings from our teacher, whom we visualize in the form of Shenlha Ökar. These five qualities are what is transmitted to us through the nectar that flows from Kuntu Zangpo through Shenlha Ökar to us.

## Trust

Often, we experience the blockage of fear, expectations, and doubts between us and our teacher. This is the main barrier that blocks us from entering into their blessing, power, and knowledge. The truth of Sanggye Tonpa Shenrab's teachings is perfect, his words are always true. But how much we benefit by practicing, visualizing, and seeking blessings depends on our capacity of trust, belief, and inspiration. Even though some particular lama may be less qualified than we think, the wisdom, compassion, and truth coming from our own practice of trust, faith, and inspiration in this lama will always give us good results. The Sanggye of the ten directions are always watching. As we see everything that lies on the table before us, in the same way they always see sentient beings, and their blessings and protection are always present.

There is a story related to this point. Once, there were several fishermen who went out to fish, but they couldn't catch anything. They were hungry and exhausted. On the way back home, they encountered a practitioner living in a cave who looked very relaxed and joyful. They thought that the difference between the hell realms and enlightened realms is here—it's the difference between them and this practitioner. And they thought they should give up their lifestyle and follow him and practice. They went to this practitioner, prostrated, and asked him: "Oh venerable lama, we are unfortunate, we were suffering, fishing, but now we have realized the lack of essence in this endless action of this cyclic existence. We would like to give up our old way of life and follow you. Please give us teachings that will liberate us and guide us to enlightenment."

The lama wasn't as qualified as they thought. He was only doing simple practices and relaxing quietly. So he started to worry, thinking about how he should answer the fishermen. He began to think in a negative way. He thought that, if he told them he didn't know the way by which such sinful people as fishermen can achieve enlightenment, he would be embarrassed. But if he agreed to lead them, he wouldn't know what to teach them. So he made a very wrong decision. He asked them, "If I give you a secret teaching, would you have the capacity to follow whatever I say?" The men said that they had made a strong decision and would do whatever he told them. He told them to hold hands and jump off the cliff into a little pond below. The fishermen didn't have much, only some fishing net and weapons. They offered all their possessions to the lama and jumped. When they jumped, before they hit the water, a manifestation came in the form of eagle. The eagle lifted them up, and they transformed into rainbow light before his eyes.

The lama became very proud. He thought that he must be really special, because he didn't give them any special teachings, but they didn't fall. They were lifted up and liberated. He thought, "If I have such power, then I should jump and liberate myself." He made a decision and stood up. But he got very attached to the offerings the men had given him, so he took the fishing net and wrapped it nicely around him. Then he jumped to the pond. Of course, he died. Moreover, he was reborn as a seagull.

If we have trust and belief without any doubt, there is a power and energy. If your faith begins to shake, it makes miracles impossible. Even though that particular lama had neither power nor wisdom to liberate the men, the Sanggye of the ten directions are always watching, and they manifested their compassion and love. Their words are always true, but we cannot experience it because of our doubt. It is the same with deities and lamas. Their blessing has no distance. In or out, day or night, it doesn't matter for them. If we are ready, their blessings are present.

The protectors and deities have no sect, no divisions. They are available equally to all sentient beings. Whoever calls them, they come. Sidpe Gyalmo is the main protector of the Bön, but many Buddhist businessmen pray to Sidpe Gyalmo. We often get offerings and requests for prayers to Sidpe Gyalmo from Buddhists. Many Buddhist travelers pray to Sidpe Gyalmo for a safe journey.

The power, wisdom and miracles of the Sanggye are always present, like the sun shining in a cloudless sky, equally for all. However, those who are in a room with no windows will not receive the sunshine; not because of the fault of the sun, but because we are hidden from it. It is the same with blessings of enlightened powers. When we are open to receive them, they appear. But we need strong, stable trust.

## Dedication

At the end of our session, we dedicate the merit of our practice to all sentient beings, so they can benefit from our practice. Dedication is very important. If we only talk about sentient beings, but we don't share our merit with them, we aren't doing what we say we should do. Everything depends on our intention. Dedication does not decrease the value or power of our practice. Dedication also develops our inner wisdom.

There is a story related with this teaching. We have a tradition of *chutor* practice, water offering. The texts say that it's the cheapest and most powerful offering. There are some prayers and visualizations, but there is a great difference in the benefit coming from this practice when we dedicate it. The power of dedication depends on our internal attitude, not just on saying the prayer. One time a high lama was doing this simple offering practice, and in his wisdom, saw hungry ghosts. He included them in his dedication and they benefited from his practice. The offering was just water, but for the hungry ghosts this was like nectar that satisfied their needs. Remember that dedication of our practice, coming deep from our heart, changes a lot for us and for others.

## The Results of Practice

If we practice lamé naljor, kyabdro, semkyed, mandala offering, and shagpa, the text says that results will appear, depending on the capacity of the practitioner.

The best practitioners will clearly develop the understanding of the importance of practice. An inspiration to practice will arise in them, which will lead them to follow the path of practice to liberation. There are also many signs of spontaneous realization of wisdom and inner qualities by the blessings of the practice of lamé naljor.

In medium level practitioners, the thought about detaching from cyclic existence and worldly life will arise. We will see the lack of essence, of truth in cyclic existence. We will realize the importance of following the path to enlightenment, and we will see all the external visions as lacking inherent existence. When these kinds of thoughts arise within us, we should immediately remember our teachers, thank them, and appreciate receiving these blessings.

The text says that this practice is like medicine for all sicknesses, achieved only by devotion, trust, and faith. By practicing, you can examine whether it's true or not. Practice without doubt and fear, and you will spontaneously experience all the signs and results. When you are doing the preliminary practices, you should practice it for at least a month, or if that is not possible, then fifteen or ten days, regularly, in a disciplined way.

We should do lamé naljor practice not only during the preliminary practice, but continue doing this practice until you achieve enlightenment. We cannot separate ourselves from the practices and blessings from the teachers until we achieve the fruit of the path of practice.

PART 2

# Ngozhi
## (the Actual Practice)

The *ngozhi*, the second part of the Fifteen-Session A-tri text, is meant to put into liberation what was awakened in the ngondro. The ngozhi has three subdivisions. The first is to recognize our mind and gain stability with the support of an object. The second is to contemplate without the support of an object (also called "objectless contemplation"). The third is the introduction to the true Nature of Mind.

# Semzin – Recognizing our Mind

## Recognizing the Mind with the Support of an Object

Traditionally, to recognize our mind and train it in how to concentrate with the support of an external object, specifically a Tibetan A syllable. Students would get up early in the morning, receive a blessing of holy water, sit on a comfortable cushion, pray to their lineage masters, and then place a Tibetan A syllable in front of them. The syllable A was chosen because it represents our mind. Traditionally, the A syllable was put on a *torma* or on a stick. The A syllable should be white, written on a dark blue background, and encircled by a rainbow. The syllable should be placed at eye level.

Today, we can easily create an A syllable with a circle of rainbow lights around it. Put the A syllable on a wall or on a stick, at eye level, so we can easily gaze on it. That's very important. Make sure the environment has no barking dogs, telephones, or other things that might disturb your concentration. It's better to practice in a quiet place, away from disturbances if possible.

This practice has three main points: body posture, eye focus, and discipline.

## Body Posture

We should sit in the five-point meditation posture, as usual. We sit cross-legged, with straight spine, and then we touch our thumbs to the base of ring finger and put our hands in meditation position. Make sure our spine is straight, because it affects our breathing and concentration. The shoulders should be slightly lifted, not tense. The neck should be slightly bent. The eyes shouldn't move up, down, left, or right—just focus on the A that is in front of us. At this moment, our body should be in perfect position. Often, when we meditate, we change our position and move, but we should avoid this, because it not only distracts us, but in group practice, also disturbs the concentration of our friends sitting around us.

Once we begin focusing and gazing at the A syllable, we should not blink, and we shouldn't care about the tears coming from our eyes, or liquid coming from our nose or mouth. Once we start gazing we should totally focus until the end of session. The three points of body, eyes, and mind should be focused on the object. We shouldn't have any other thoughts or care for other things. Keeping this posture helps us to stabilize our inner elements, to relax our physical body, and gives us more openness and stability. By straightening our spine, we control our inner channels and winds. Blood, breath, and waters move through our channels, and by keeping our posture, their circulation will recover to the normal state. When we practice, it's good to place a towel on our lap, because saliva and other liquids may leak from our mouth, nose, or eyes. With time, it will stop by itself, but to protect our clothes we may want to use a towel. And during the practice we should let everything flow, we shouldn't care about this. We should think only about the A.

Generally, this practice should be done for at least seven days. Divide each day into either four or six practice sessions. We should practice as much as our time allows, trying at all times to be disciplined.

## Eye Focus

When we look at the object, our rigpa (awareness) must be focused one-pointedly with the A syllable in front of us. Our eyes are looking at the object, and our awareness also has to be focused on it. Gongdzod Ritrod Chenpo says that if we open our eyes too wide, our mind will be wild, and it will not stabilize. If our eyes are too closed, it will lead us to dullness and sleep. So, the eyes should be neither too opened, nor too closed. They should be opened normally and focused. Once we begin to focus, we shouldn't move our eyes, we shouldn't blink, but only focus on the A. During our sessions, we may feel some irritation of the eyes, perhaps a burning sensation. We may feel an urge to close our eyes, but we should not. Even when tears fill our eyes and we cannot see the A clearly, it doesn't matter. We should maintain our concentration.

The text says that we should focus like when we try to thread a needle, or as an archer focuses on a target when he shoots. We should focus without being distracted by other things we see; we should focus only on our target. Our eyes and mind shouldn't be distracted by other sounds or visions. They should be fully concentrated on the A. We also shouldn't think of the past, plan the future, or think about the present. We shouldn't follow any such disturbances to our concentration, but rather focus on the A without any distractions. We should be fully present, with sharp focus, without wavering—like a straight stick, or like water flowing through an iron pipe—straightforward, with force of energy, awareness, and presence. Our focus should be like a bowstring, full of potential energy. Our focus is so strong and well-grounded that our body is like a dead body, without any other thoughts, without any distractions, no matter what sound or vision appears and without any dullness. We have to be present moment after moment, without anything else distracting us.

# Discipline

The third point is discipline, referring to the physical position of our body during practice. The text says we should not move our eyelids, eyes, or body. For beginners, even swallowing saliva may be distracting. That's why we must let everything come out. Whatever happens, let it happen. The session shouldn't be too long at the beginning, just as long as it takes to complete one circle of *trengwa* (prayer beads) of the MA TRI or DU TRI SU nyenpa. At first, we should do shorter sessions. Then, gradually, we can expand the time of our meditation. The more we are familiar with our meditation practice, the longer time we can practice. We should practice for about a week, until we get signs of success in the practice. When we practice every day, regularly, to receive signs, we can use other objects than the A syllable. We can use some images of Sanggye, Shenlha Ökar, or other religious symbols, whatever is comfortable for you. But normally we focus on the A syllable, because it has a deeper meaning.

## Signs of Progress in the Semzin Practice

When we practice, we may get signs that we are gaining stability in our concentration and experiences in our meditation. Some people can have the signs very quickly, perhaps in the first session, on the first day. Many people may experience these signs after three or four days, or perhaps a bit longer.

We are seeking *semzin* (concentration and realization of our mind). It's important to be careful in every session not to get distracted or get lost in stability without focus. We must make sure we never lose our focus and not let our minds wander.

## The Use of Sounds as an Alternate Practice

If we practice in the way described in the text, and even after putting effort into trying, we haven't achieved any signs of realization and stability, we should do a practice using sound. Go, with your friends or alone, to a high, quiet place, like the top of a mountain or the roof of a house. If you're with friends, they should sit around you. The text says that if you are alone with no friends, then put several heavy Tibetan woolen cloaks around you, so it seems like you are sitting with your companions sitting around you. Sit in the same body posture, eyes looking up into space, and then chant HUNG HRI, HUNG HUNG or HING HING sounds. Our eyes should be gazing up, and our awareness should follow our eyes. Our awareness should be integrated with our gaze. We should chant more than one hundred, but less than one thousand times. According to this text, if we practice this way, we will surely achieve stability and realize our mind. This technique of pronouncing sound is for older, blind, or very calm people. Some people have a very peaceful, calm nature; this technique is especially beneficial for them.

## Inner Signs of Progress

When our mind is trained to focus and concentrate, and we realize our mind, then inner and outer signs appear. When our awareness is well stabilized, we may get eight kinds of feelings, which are signs of development of the practice. These are:

1. Like a turtle put in a large basin remains unmoving, just as it was placed in the basin, the practitioner remains in the state of meditation, without shifting his focus, without changing his concentration.

2. Like a little bird shivering in cold weather or hail, the practitioner feels an inner vibration, like shivering from cold, even when the physical body doesn't move. At that moment, when our awareness is strictly focused, we experience this vibration involuntarily.

3. Like grapes thrown on a flat surface lie still and on the same level, the practitioner's body and mind are balanced and relaxed, with the experience of internal peace and calm.

4. Like trying to set fire with flint, sometimes we succeed and sometimes we do not, the practitioner sometimes feels focused and still, and sometimes not. Our stability comes and goes.

5. Like water passing through an iron pipe, straight and full of energy, the practitioner focuses without any distractions, in one constant stream of awareness, without going faster or

slower. And like water going through a pipe straight to its goal, our awareness at once goes with full energy straight to the object of concentration.

6.   Like a bee on a flower gets attached to the flower when it finds the nectar and doesn't try to separate from it, so the practitioner, once he gets focused and is completely stable, has no will to end the session. The awareness remains in the practice without any will to finish it.

7.   Like a fish swimming in the water, without any barriers or difficulties, without any thoughts, without effort or problem, the practitioner, when he or she focuses on the object, encounters no distracting thoughts or intentions. We are focusing without any barriers or blockages; it's natural, spontaneous, like a fish swimming in the water. The fish is never beyond the water, it never comes out of the water. In the same way, our awareness stays with our concentration on the A syllable, and deeper inside.

8.   Like a soft wind that touches the trees as it blows but leaves no print or trace, when the practitioner focuses, he or she is completely concentrated. If thoughts arise, they will not affect your focus, and you will remain calm and at peace. There is no grasping of the A syllable. No matter how much we have integrated our awareness with it, we have no attachment to it, we leave no print.

All these examples describe what our experience will be like. If we only think analytically about these examples, we will not make any real progress. These examples show not how we should think, but how we feel.

We may have all of these signs, or only one or two. The appearance of these signs confirms that our practice is going well and that we are stabilizing in our meditation. But we should not expect these signs. These are the inner signs of success in our practice. This practice of *zhine* (calm abiding) not only gives us stability of mind; it also leads us to realize our true Nature of Mind.

## Outer Signs of Progress

What are the outer signs that we may experience through practicing concentration on the A syllable?

1.  We may experience that we are unable to move our body once we enter the meditation position.

2.  We may unintentionally and spontaneously laugh, or cry, or jump up, or do some other unusual physical activity. These may appear naturally, without intention. It may seem strange, when you are among other people, to suddenly jump, dance, and laugh. People may think you are crazy, but instead it is a sign of progress in your practice.

3.  We may feel dizziness and nausea.

4.  We may feel we are unable to close our eyes; we may start to worry that something is wrong with our eyes. Actually, nothing is wrong with our eyes, but we can also remain in practice as long as we want. At the beginning we felt like we needed to blink, but now we have overcome the need to blink, and we can gaze as long as we want.

5.  We may lose feeling in our legs or feel that all our body is numb. We may sweat, like we're out in the sun, or like we are working hard. Our body may shake a little bit. While sitting, we may also fall over on our side. If we see someone falling on their side during practice, we shouldn't wake this person by shaking him or her or by using force; we can wake him or her gently and softly, throw a little rice on him or her or sprinkle some blessing water. This happens and is nothing to worry about. Just be aware that this may happen.

These signs are a normal result of our practice. These signs indicate that the inner elements of our body are normalizing and settling, so we become calmer and more stable. When our thoughts are too active and agitated, it means that our inner winds are too active and disturb us. We have a lot of channels through which energy circulates. In our central channel, different wheels are situated. When inner elements are aroused, they disturb our awareness. As in the outside world, when a strong wind comes, it carries away everything that is not stable. In the same way, our inner elements move our thoughts and disturb them. By sitting in meditation position and practicing, we normalize our functioning, especially our inner winds.

Our inner and outer elements are related, and we rely on all of them. When the external elements are polluted, it affects us. Scientist today speak of cleaning our environment not only because it affects the outside world, but because it affects human beings. By doing these practices, we are returning to our normal state. And when our winds calm down, everything settles.

We have to understand that focusing on the A syllable not only gives us stability, but also leads us to realizing our mind, the true Nature of Mind. There are traditions that focus mainly on stability, ignoring other aspects of this practice. This is also good. This is a kind of *zhine*. Remember, *zhi* means "peace" or "calm," and *ne* means "remaining." We are remaining in the peace of our concentration, our thoughts.

In the Bön tradition, we experience this stable abiding, but we go beyond that. This practice is an introduction, a method to discover the nature of our mind. Only with this stability can we discover the nature of our mind. If we didn't know what our mind is, nobody could explain it to us. If we don't understand our mind, then there is no point in talking about the Nature of Mind. This method leads not only to stability, but also gives us introduction to the Nature of Mind. It's important to know that.

By practicing we learn how to stabilize our active thoughts and bring them to a state of calm and peace. Then we can remain in meditation longer, without distractions from the physical body and from our mind. We can remain as long as we want in the state of focus, no matter what we are focusing on. It can be the natural state of mind, the mind of enlightenment, or compassion, or lamé naljor practice. When our mind is not stable, our focus is not clear, and our focus doesn't have the energy required. If we are trying to meditate on Tapihritsa, for example, with an unstable mind, then we find that, moment after moment, thoughts spontaneously arise and distract our concentration on Tapihritsa. Sometimes we even lose focus and can no longer contemplate lamé naljor.

When we have practiced *zhine* well and achieved stability, it helps us to remain the way we want, where we want. When we have developed the force of *zhine*, we can change the object of our focus, and our mind will stay on that object. This helps us to practice, to meditate. When we meditate on the natural state of mind, we can remain in meditation without any distractions as long as we want. We extend the length of our meditation. And the longer we meditate, the more we grow, and the more results we achieve. This is our aim.

In Tibet during the time of cultural revolution there lived a well-known great master, Nyima Rinpoche from the Khyungpo area. He was a simple monk and a good practitioner. He developed his practice well. During the cultural revolution, he disappeared. People didn't know where he went. He went to a cave on a mountain and meditated there. He took only a small bag of *tsampa* (ground roasted barley), a wooden bowl and a little kettle to boil water. He went to the cave, made himself some tea, and entered meditation. He never even drank his tea. He meditated for a very long time. Some people say he spent fifteen years in meditation; others say it was only seven. But he spent at least seven years in meditation.

After this time, some shepherds found him and told the local villagers. People came to him and forced him to come with them. He couldn't stand up because of all the years in cross-legged position. His nails had grown into his hands, and his hair was very long. On his wooden bowl, there was only a trace of evaporated tea, and his little bag of *tsampa* was lying there, just as when he brought it, which turned to dust when someone touched it. He remained in meditation without any food; he entered a deep state of mind and didn't require food.

The officers didn't believe him. They forced him to eat, but he got sick. They put a special person to watch over him, put him in a prison, and he practiced in prison as if he were in a cave and didn't eat anything. Even the officers closely watching him were inspired and wondered what to do with him. They saw he was not eating, he didn't require food, and he could stay in meditation as long as he wanted. They freed him, saying that, because he didn't require food, he had gone beyond the human condition, and so he was beyond their rule. And he went and kept meditating. After a few years the situation changed a bit for the better, giving more religious freedom. People started building monasteries and practicing, and then he began to travel to many Bönpo sites in Eastern Tibet, in Kham and Amdo. There were no teachers or established monasteries in those areas, so he encouraged people to rebuild the monasteries that had been destroyed. He gave many teachings and transmissions to connect the younger generation. He ordained many monks. He recognized many tulkus (reincarnated holy persons) to lead the monasteries in places where there was no lama. He did many other great things and became a lamp of teachings. He kept the teachings, practiced them, and spread them. He was respected as a great *drub-chen* ("accomplished one," who realizes the truth of cyclic existence) all over Tibet for the work he did for Bön.

We can also achieve such results. They come from practice, and there is no reason we couldn't be like that. He was just an ordinary monk. Through practice he became a great teacher, and he spread the teachings. He passed away when he was still young, very unfortunately for Bön and for all sentient beings.

The inner and outer signs we have mentioned depend on our inner elements. If we have an excess of the water and earth elements, then the stability and recognition of our mind may come later, but they will also be better supported later; the stability will remain longer. If our fire and wind elements are more energetic, then it will be easy to achieve stability in the beginning, but it will be more difficult to maintain stability, and we will be prone to interference and disturbance.

If the beginning of our meditation session is clearer and easier, and by the end of our meditation it gets more difficult, that may indicate that in our past life we have received these teachings, but we didn't practice seriously. We might have disrespected the practices. It takes a long time to achieve stabilization again, so practitioners must practice with the support of an object, such as the A syllable, very seriously and enthusiastically, making sure they have gained a good result of stability.

If the beginning of our session is difficult, we are agitated and not stable, but gradually it improves, that is a sign that we are new to this type of practice, and our further development will be easier. If we find it hard to focus with the support of an object, but easier to contemplate without an object, this may be caused by other reasons. If both the practice with an object and without object is easy for us, it means that we have a good connection from our past lives, and we are continuing our practice. It's a good sign showing that we have a good capacity for practice and a strong link with past life.

## The Search for the Self

Early in the morning and late in the evening, when we cannot see the support object clearly, we should search ourselves, meaning contemplate and look within for our mind. We are always focused on "I" and "me." Now, go into yourself and analyze: Who is creating this view? Who has this sense of presence of "I?" Look for it. It's the source of our anger, attachment, ignorance, jealousy, pride, as well as all negativities, suffering, and even happiness we experience in this life. Everything happens because of this "self." This self-mindedness causes us to get caught up in making divisions between positive and negative, good and bad, self and others. We create divisions within our group, our sangha, our community, and our country. Because of this "self" or "I," we destroy our unity.

Who makes this "I?" It's so strong, energetic, and powerful. It dictates our life. We have to find out where it comes from, where it stays, and where it goes. We should think, contemplate. Where is this strong "I" and "me," the source of all these actions and events? We must go into ourselves and search. What does it look like? What is its color? What size is it? The "I" must be there. The "I" determines whether we react positively or negatively to something. We do everything the way this "I" tells us to.

It's time to identify who dictates our lives. Until now, we have done everything only because it told us to, not because we understood this "I." Now, we should try to find it, to realize it. Is there anything to realize? Does anything exist there, as we perceive it, as we react to it?

When we look for our self, we must be careful not to get trapped by our thoughts. When we use our mind to search for our self, we are using thoughts to search for thoughts.

It's not easy to find the "I." We won't find anything in just one moment. It takes a while to even start searching properly. But if we do this searching practice regularly, then we will discover whether this "I" exists as we thought or not. According to our experience, we will come to some conclusion. We may either say that "I" doesn't exist, or that it exists and it looks a certain way, or that we didn't find anything. In result of our practice of searching, we should have some discovery.

In the early days in Tibet, lamas used different ways to help students to discover themselves and to identify their Nature of Mind (*rang ngo tödpa*). The lama would advise students to practice looking into themselves for a month and then come back and report what was understood or discovered—what the mind looks like. This is the way we practice it now. We search for our mind, and then we come back to the teacher who gave us the introduction to our mind and give our report. Otherwise, we are not able to achieve this realization. It is easy to become confused, and we encounter many doubts in our practice.

People have different experiences and discoveries. I have seen that some people searched for their minds for months. After the search, some people came back with colorful stones, some brought back flowers, some came with dried horse stool. They showed these things to the lama, saying that this is what their mind really looks like.

In Dolanji, when I was a student, there was an old man who was practicing this. He had finished his preliminary practices, received *phowa*, and was searching for his mind. At the back of our temple there is a nice place, from where you have a beautiful overview of the village. I often went there in the evening before our evening debates to sit there and memorize my texts. This old man would circumambulate the temple in the evening, and he used to go to this place to rest. Whenever he came to this place, I didn't learn, and he didn't circumambulate; we just sat and chatted. We were wasting our time there, actually.

One day I asked him what practice he was doing. He told me he was searching for his mind. He said that it was really funny, he was amused and excited. He said: "My 'I' is there; it's a little boy, very cute. He comes from one place on my body and goes to another.

When I look at him, he looks back at me, and when I just carelessly leave him, he goes away. He is a naked little cute boy." He was thinking his "I" was a little boy, very agitated, always moving, who often moves into his hand, because then they could both see each other. This is how the old man identified himself. He was serious, and thought this was his "I."

We don't know how it happens, that we decide what is our mind, our "I." In a strange and funny way, we make a decision that yes, this is "I." This is how we bind ourselves. We are bound by all these thoughts in our daily life. We live our whole life bound by our thoughts, and depending on these thoughts, we are active, busy, grasping, so-called happy, so-called suffering, and so-called disappointed. Everything that happens to us happens because of our thoughts. I don't know what the old man's final discovery was after he went to his teacher and clarified his experience. We never talked about it.

We need to have time to practice and search; we need to identify ourselves. If we don't identify ourselves, then we don't have any foundation to practice. Only on the base of real discovery of our self, of our mind, can we develop our practice and understanding. If we don't discover our mind, how can we practice the natural state of mind? If we don't have a good foundation, how can we build a nine-story house? Each and every aspect of our wisdom and knowledge has to have a foundation in practice. If we don't have this base, it's very hard to discover our true nature.

Why is Dzogchen the highest teaching among the Nine Ways? Dzogchen talks about mind and the Nature of Mind. It is specific, detailed, clear. It deals with direct perception of the mind and the Nature of Mind. Other teachings, like Madhyamaka (dho), and ngag, have different levels of understanding the Nature of Mind, and different ways of discovering the Nature of Mind, but they are indirect methods, not based on direct perception. Therefore, we consider them as lower. Only Dzogchen leads to the discovery of the true Nature of Mind.

The method of searching our mind is not the ultimate method of Dzogchen practice. It is a method of bringing ourselves to the Nature of Mind. We cannot find our Nature of Mind; Dzogchen is beyond searching, beyond limits. But this method is like a key that we may use to open the door to practice. The key is only a tool to get into the house. When we enter a house, we use the key to open the door. Once we're inside the house, we look at the inside of the house; we don't look at the key. But the key is the method to enter the house. Without it, we wouldn't be able to see the beauty of the house. Similarly, we will not find anything through the method of searching our mind, but it allows us to enter into the nature of our mind. If we know how to search, if we spend time on it and go into it in a detailed way, this will lead us to achieving realization.

The process of searching our mind is carried out by our deluded thoughts. When we say that we are searching, meditating, and trying to find our mind, we are producing thoughts. We produce thoughts like, "What is the mind? Where does it come from? Where does it go? What does it look like?" And our conclusion, "This is the natural state; this is the 'me' that I have found," is also a thought. We use a thought to define and start our search; we search using thoughts; and the conclusion is also a thought. We are bound by thoughts.

This thought-bound meditation is not our goal. We spend time on this practice to gain more experience. When we have the opportunity, we can clarify any doubts we have with a teacher, so that we can change our path if necessary and get good results. We must follow the instructions of the teachings very carefully. These teachings are not just a common lecture. Through them, we are trying to transform our reality and understanding, and liberate ourselves from dualistic thoughts. This will develop our wisdom in this life and bring us benefit in future rebirths.

We shouldn't waste time wondering if the practice works or not. Follow the teachings carefully. Don't lose your enthusiasm for searching until you have a good experience and understanding. Keep practicing as your teacher advises from his own experience of receiving understanding, and you will receive the same. Don't stop part way through the process and decide to practice something else; if we do, we will not achieve anything we can confidently hold on to when we are dying. This is important.

If we have problems focusing on our search for our mind, the text says we should practice taking refuge, guru yoga, or other practices. For some people, a practice using chanting and sound works better than the meditation we are discussing. Chanting is a way to bring us into the meaning of the prayer. When we chant, at the same time we reflect on the meaning of the chant. When our chanting ends, we continue to hold the meaning in our minds.

What we chant is not the important thing; the essence of the practice is what matters.

We pray to our root teacher, seeking clarification and protection from external, internal, and secret obstacles. If we are devoted to our root teacher and pray without hesitation or doubts, there are many possibilities of change and transformation. These changes will happen within you, without you knowing how they happen. Wisdom and understanding will flourish inside you. If you don't understand something in the morning, and then you pray from your heart, it is possible that in the evening you will understand it. Such things happen by the blessing of the Sanggye, teaching protectors, and teachers. But to experience such things, we need to have complete devotion, without doubt, without wondering whether we will have such an experience or not. Doubt is only thing that is blocking it. When we are standing on a crossroads wondering which way we should go, we can waste all our time choosing whether to go right or left. We should make a decision and go in that direction without doubt. If a needle had two points, you wouldn't be able to sew with it. And if you have doubts, you won't be able to make a decision and reach your goal. In Tibet, we have a saying: "A mind with two thoughts will not achieve its goal; a needle with two points cannot sew."

After we have searched for our mind and have experienced something that makes us think we have discovered our mind, we should report this to our teacher and ask for additional instructions. The text says that after searching, reporting to the teacher, and discussing with him, we begin to notice the true quality of our mind and of ourselves.

## Stories of Searching for Our Mind

The Fifteen-Session A-tri text contains a separate section of six little stories or examples, illustrating our true mind and ourselves. The author of the A-tri text says he has added these stories because he found them helpful in the search for his mind.

### 1. The Lost Prince

The first story is about a kingdom ruled by an old king who had two sons, two princes. When the old king died, the elder son was enthroned. The younger boy disappeared in a crowd. After a while, the older son passed away, and there was no one to rule the kingdom and sit on the golden throne. The ministers knew that the younger prince had disappeared years ago, so they decided to look for him so that he could rule the kingdom. They felt confident they could identify the boy when they found him, because they knew he had distinctive marks on his body: on his shoulders, he had sun and moon signs, and on his thigh, he had an image of dice used for divination.

The ministers sent people to search for the boy. When they found the boy, they blessed him with holy water and performed other purification rituals. Then, they gave him prince's robes to wear and enthroned him. The young prince ruled the kingdom, and the country was filled with joy again.

The inner meaning of the story is this: The two brothers, two princes, one who ruled and one who was lost, means that both the enlightened ones and the ordinary sentient beings have the same base. Being lost in the crowd symbolizes us, the sentient beings who have not achieved self-realization. We are lost in the crowd of khorwa, and we do not sit on the throne of the real state. Finding the son and enthroning him symbolizes our achievement of enlightenment—of the throne of the natural state. The minister, who is looking for the lost king, is the lama, the teacher. The sun and moon signs on his shoulders are characteristics of the natural state, clarity, and emptiness. The divination dice symbolize two different aspects of khorwa and *nyangde* ("one who is beyond suffering," or has achieved enlightenment) while circling in khorwa. The blessing water, the purification ritual, and the change of clothes symbolize the preliminary practices that we perform to purify ourselves in order to overcome negativities and achieve realization. The enthronement is the symbol of achieving realization, the state of enlightenment.

## 2. The Nature of Our Face

We all have a face, and our face has never been separated from us. But we are not able to see our face ourselves; we need the help of a mirror. Similarly, our Nature of Mind has never been separated from us, but it's hidden from us, so we have never realized it, never discovered it. We can only discover it by instructions and introduction from the teacher. As we need a mirror to see our face, we need the instructions and guidance of a teacher to discover the nature of our mind.

### 3. The Story of O Dze

The third example is a man named O Dze, whose name means "Beautiful Light." But he has many other names and titles, depending on the person who speaks with him. Some people call him, "Uncle O Dze," others call him, "brother," his parents call him, "son," and so on. Each person calls him by a different name, depending on their relationship to him and their view of him. Everyone sees him differently, but he is the same man.

Similarly, we have one base, one nature, one essence. It's a single point, *nelug thigle nyagchik*. We give it different names, such as "the nature of the base, "the nature of the path",", "the nature of the result" and others. These are definitions given from the perspective of our level of practice. But from the viewpoint of our nature, there is no base, no path, no result; just total oneness.

### 4. The Sesame Seeds

The fourth example talks about sesame seeds. Sesame seeds are filled with oil, and by crushing them, we can extract the oil. Every sesame seed is fully filled with oil. Each seed has the full potential to give oil. In the same way, each of us has his or her own nature, the potential to be a Sanggye. All of our natures are the same. But if we don't practice, we will not discover our nature. So, although we have this potential, we will never manifest it without practice. The texts say that if we discover our nature, we are enlightened; if we don't discover it, we are deluded, and we keep circling in cyclic existence. Enlightenment is not far from us; it's within us. We're not looking for anything that isn't already there; we're just trying to discover what is there already. Dzogchen tries to discover our nature, not to create something new. It shows us what we haven't seen before, but that was in us all the time. We discover our Nature of Mind by practice, but we are not creating anything new.

## 5. The Lamp in the Pot

The fifth example talks about a butter lamp in a clay pot. The clay pot symbolizes our physical body, the butter lamp in the clay pot is our consciousness. When the light of the butter lamp comes through the top of the clay pot, it is a reflection of our Nature of Mind. The nature of our mind has an aspect of clarity and the ability to reflect, to shine. When we practice properly, we can see the light of the five elements, the rainbow light, and we can manifest it as a symbol of our practice.

## 6. The Imprisoned King

The sixth example speaks of a country that had two kings. Each king had three ministers in their court, five foreign affairs ministers, 61 messengers and 84,000 soldiers. One of these two kings was very good, and the other was bad. They were often in conflict, arguing with each other, but the bad king was always victorious. One of the ministers proposed to set an ambush on the road where the bad king and his soldiers would pass. Since the bad king always led his army, they could catch him and thus conquer his army. The ministers and soldiers carefully prepared the ambush, and when they saw the bad king leading his soldiers, they caught him. Once they had conquered the bad king, his soldiers were subdued, and there were no more challenges from them.

The one country symbolizes each of us. The two kings are awareness (*rigpa yeshe*) and ignorance (*marigpa*). The three ministers are the three poisons, and their positive counterparts, which are the three enlightened bodies (*bönku, dzogku,* and *tulku;* Sanskrit *dharmakaya, sambhogakaya, nirmanakaya*). The five foreign ministers are the five poisons and five wisdoms. The sixty-one messengers are known as the sixty-one wisdoms and sixty-one emotional defilements. The 84,000 soldiers are the 84,000 doors to teachings, or 84,000 emotions. The king of ignorance is the main source of all our suffering and negativities. The good king represents awareness, which subdues the darkness of ignorance. We are like this kingdom, and once we conquer our ignorance, then automatically all that is caused by ignorance is cleared. When the bad king is caught, all his soldiers are subdued.

We should apply the meaning of these examples to our practice in our daily life. If we have difficulties with searching our mind, or if we find it difficult to begin the search, then it may be helpful to reflect on these stories and their meaning, and apply this meaning in us. It will help us to practice searching for our mind. The text says that these six stories were very useful in the author's experience, and so he included them for our benefit.

# What If We Can't Find Our Mind?

We have seen the instructions of the A-tri text for searching for our mind using an external object and also using sound. What should we do if we still cannot find our mind? The text says that our inability to identify or understand our mind with these practices means we are not ready at the moment for the introduction to the nature of our mind.

In this case, we need to return to some of the basic practices, including shagpa (confession), lamé naljor, and prayers to the Three Jewels and to our lineage masters. We should also go to high, well-known lamas to receive some empowerments and blessings, to remove obstacles, and open more internal space and wisdom.

Then we may try to realize our mind again, starting with the practice of stabilizing the mind with the support of an object, trying to stabilize it and to understand it. This time, we can also use different stabilizing objects. For example, instead of the A syllable, we could use an image of Shenlha Ökar. We can also practice breathing methods and physical exercises to remove obstacles. The text says it's important to have enthusiasm and not get discouraged. We should practice with hope and energy. We shouldn't think that we will fail. Instead, we should be convinced that we are going to succeed. We need this self-confidence and energy. If others could do it, why shouldn't we? The only reason is that our practice is not strong enough. If one week is not enough, then we should practice for a second and third week, and then a month. If we are still not getting the result, we should try another way.

There are many practitioners who remain in stability of mind but don't achieve realization. In that case, they go to high, well-known teachers of their school (whether it is dho (Madhyamaka or sutra), ngag (tantra) or sem (Dzogchen)) for advice. They talk with these teachers about their practice, privately, not in public, because these are personal experiences. It's always good to go to your teacher privately for clarification, or for another method, or for other guidance.

Most of all, we need enthusiasm. If we practice enthusiastically, we will definitely achieve our goal. It's only a matter of whether we have the strength to practice without getting discouraged, without giving up. The great masters from early times have said that the depth of blessings and powers of blessing affect the disciple according to his capacity, to how the teacher has instructed him, and to how energetically he practices. These things all determine when we will achieve realization, but it's only a matter of if we achieve it sooner or later. As long as we practice continually without giving up, we will achieve realization.

The gradual path to realization that we have discussed is the most common way. There are also some rare, special cases. Some students may achieve realization in miraculous ways, very fast. Sometimes a teacher is very violent towards his students, and may beat them. The thigh bone used in *chö* practice often has a leather whip, to cast the demons out of student. Great lamas have performed such actions towards sick people in many cases. Real *chö* practitioners behave differently than ordinary people; you never know what they will do. When you meet a *chö* practitioner, and he beats you, you must bow down with gratitude. It's considered good luck, because by hitting you he removes your negativities and obstacles.

There is a story in the A-tri lineage of Togdhen Gomchen Barwa, a well-known practitioner and *togdhen* (master or yogi). In his early life he was travelling and doing business, but then he decided to give up everything and he became a practitioner. In the early times in Tibet, that wasn't so easy. If your lama lived in seclusion, there was often nobody around, so the disciple had no way to get food. When his supplies ran out, he had to go to a nearby village to beg for food. When he was practicing, he was doing well, but he would have to stop his practice for weeks or months to go get food.

He complained to his teacher that he was losing his meditation experiences because of this. His teacher told him there was another method to introduce him to the nature of his mind. The teacher took him to a slippery meadow and told him to run through the meadow. And Togdhen Barwa ran and slipped on the grass, fell down, hit his head, and lost consciousness. When he woke up, he saw his teacher laughing at him, and at that moment, he realized his natural state of mind.

The text says that this method, stabilizing our mind with an external object, is for calming us down and bringing us to the state of peace. It's important to practice enthusiastically. Inner and outer signs of achieving stability should appear in three to four days. We should continue to practice enthusiastically until we get a result.

SESSION 6

# Concentration Without the Support of a Material Object

The sixth of the 15 sessions begins with a prostration to the lama, our root teacher.

This session has two subdivisions. The first is contemplation with no object of support; the second is contemplation in the state of calmness, zhine. In the fifth session, we discussed ways to concentrate and develop stability of our mind, using the support of a material object, like the A syllable, through sound, and through other techniques. In this session, we don't use any material object. Instead, we concentrate by contemplating with no supporting object.

The first subdivision has four points: body posture; eye gazing; relaxing the mind; and discipline.

## Body Posture

When we meditate, we sit in the five or seven-point body posture. The five-point body posture is more common. We cross our legs, with hands resting on our lap, straight spine, slightly, naturally bent neck, and proper eye gazing. In the seven-point posture, in addition to the normal five points, the stomach should be drawn in towards the spine, and the tongue touches the upper pallet.

To sit in meditation posture, we sit on a comfortable cushion, so we can sit with no force, no pressure. We relax without concentrating on the body or getting distracted by it. Our body should be like a dead body, with no movement. Even though we need to hold the posture, we shouldn't force ourselves to hold it by applying pressure. Our concentration should not be distracted by our body posture. That's why it's important to sit in the right position before we start meditating. Once we begin meditating, if we start thinking about pain somewhere, or itching, or feeling uncomfortable, we may develop the habit of thinking about pain, and it will always bother us and disturb our concentration. So we sit in the correct position from the very beginning. And once we sit, we just sit and mediate. No matter what is going on with our body, we just sit and meditate. Then internal and external conditions don't distract us. We will be able to bring our channels and winds to normal positions, all our *khorlo* (chakras) and body structures to their natural state. Then, our visualization, or concentration, or whatever we are focusing on, is right. When our channels are not stabilized, not settled, and when our inner winds are not settled, then it distracts us and disturbs our concentration; the imbalance of these inner winds disturbs and agitates us, so we become distracted. Our purpose is developing non-dual and non-distracted concentration, a non-distracted awareness, so that we can remain still and focused on the object of our meditation.

This posture will help us realize that from our first birth in the universe until now, we have taken many forms in different times and different circumstances. Each time, we had a different body, but we have never gained anything from it. Rather, we have cultivated only distractions, suffering, unpleasant states, and depression. The essence of practice is also in realizing that everything we have cultivated until now all went in the wrong direction. So, now we must be tired of our mistakes, which causes us to remain in this cyclic existence. We must realize what we should cultivate and how to cultivate it. Our body posture will support this realization.

## Eye Gazing

There are certain ways of gazing when we meditate. The wrathful form of gazing is when our eyes are directed upwards. The peaceful form of gazing, or gazing like a *yungdrung sempa* (bodhisattva), is with our eyes looking downwards slightly and naturally. Most of the thangka paintings, images of buddhas, statues etc. have eyes in the peaceful gazing position. We can also meditate directing our eyes to the right or to the left. Gazing to the right symbolizes method or compassion, and gazing to the left symbolizes wisdom, which realizes the true state of mind.

But here we use none of these methods; we are using the way that the greatly realized masters, *rigdzins* or *sempas*, and enlightened ones used when they were contemplating. They just looked straight ahead into space, without moving, without moving their eyes or eyelids. We simply gaze, looking straight, into space, without any movement, without blinking.

When we look directly into space, our rigpa (awareness) has to be focused on the space where our eyes are gazing. The empty aspect of that space should be the center of the concentration of our rigpa. According to one of the great past masters, if we learn how to gaze into space in an extraordinary way, it will make us superior and distinct from khorwa, and we will gain extraordinary essential realization. The purpose of the practice of gazing into space is not simply to spend time, to see different visions and objects. True, once you begin gazing into space, visions of different objects appear, like lights, shadows, and others; but our purpose is not to watch these visions. The purpose is that our rigpa should be absorbed into the essence of the space where we are gazing. This way we realize the inseparable nature of inner and outer space.

# Relaxing the Mind

The third point is to concentrate our mind and bring it to a state of relaxation, without activating it, and without being disturbed by the arising thoughts. We have to realize that, until now, we have been born many times. Each time, we were born with a mind, very active, distinguishing good from bad, thinking dualistically. Our mind consciousness has generated many levels of thoughts: good, bad, neutral, positive; but none of these thoughts has ever helped us to liberate from this suffering of cyclic existence. The action of our mind, generating varieties of karma, causes us to be born in this form of life and to continue the same experiences. We don't achieve the real essence of our Nature of Mind by all the thoughts and activities of the mind. We should realize that first.

We should also realize that the mind is the source of both suffering and pleasure. Now, the time has come for us to transform and correct it. Each of these practices is meant to bring us benefit and to liberate us from suffering, to achieve enlightenment. To do that, we need to properly understand our situation. We must make a commitment that, at last, we are fed up with those result-less activities. Now, we should engage in actions that have positive results.

When we begin to meditate, we should not get distracted by thoughts that arise. Thoughts arise naturally. Whatever arises within its own base, we simply watch it, with the presence of awareness, without following the thought or getting distracted by it. We should remain focused, present, and aware.

127

## Kunzhi, Rigpa, and Unification

Rigpa, the son, is our awareness. Kunzhi is the base of all, the mother nature of all space. In Dzogchen, *kunzhi* is short for *kunzhi jang chub kyi sem*. Kunzhi is not the mind itself, but the true Nature of Mind. Kunzhi is the mother, and rigpa is the son. In essence, the son, rigpa, integrates into kunzhi without modifying anything, without distractions or illusions. When we realize our Nature of Mind, it is like the son recognizing his mother and the mother recognizing her son. Without any interference from doubt or expectations, they just directly realize each other and rest fully in that realization, like the son resting in the mother's lap.

When we realize and unify with our rigpa and rest in the state of kunzhi, then we are contemplating our Nature of Mind. But when we make efforts to achieve this by "practicing," immediately we begin to get distracted. Without any plans or expectations, one thought comes after another, spontaneously. When we are able to contemplate, we are beyond doubts, expectations and dualistic thoughts, beyond any material support. When we are in that state, material objects don't have any effect on us. They don't bother or disturb us. There is nothing to do, so we remain at peace. Therefore, when we contemplate the natural state of mind, our five senses will not distract us. That is the stable state.

Gongdzo Ritrod Chenpo writes that when contemplating without the support of a material object, we should just be relaxed, free, and present. Then we will experience something extraordinary. Both dho and ngag teachings also say we should keep everything naturally in the state, cutting off all expectations and doubts and freeing from all activities, uniting in the oneness of a single sphere, integrating into the space of emptiness, and leaving everything in its own state. This is unifying rigpa with kunzhi. When we concentrate with presence, without any distractions, in the state of our awareness, then certain experiences will come. These experiences are not described; that is done purposely, so we don't expect them. The experiences will arise, and having certain experiences signifies we have realized certain things. We should discuss our experiences with our teacher to get guidance on what these experiences mean for us.

## Developing Zhine

The word *zhine* comes from two Tibetan words. *Zhi* means "base," "peace," or "calm." In this case, the base is our true nature of mind. *Ne* means "remaining" or "abiding." This means our thoughts are remaining in the true base of our mind, in peace, and are abiding in the calm state of our mind.

One of the main dho texts says that when we are in a non-dual state without any distractions, this is called *zhine*, stability. Continuing that meditation with no physical or mental distractions, with no difficulty, without getting tired, is called the result of the practice of stability of concentration. When we are able to concentrate without any distractions, then we will achieve the stability and realization of the state of zhine. As a result of that zhine lasting for a long time, we will achieve true stability of body and mind. We say that after training in zhine well, we will experience perfect stability of mind and body. Then, we can be in meditation as long as we want, with no difficulties created by body or mind.

The distractions and disturbances we experience in meditation, according to this text, can be divided into two categories. The first distraction is the concept of subject and object. Normally we all perceive the world in categories of subject and object. When we see something, it's "me" seeing that particular thing. When you see me, and I see you, we both have this particular view of, "I see you." One looks, and one is seen. We should not think about who looks, or who is seen, who meditates, or what the object of meditation is. We should not hold this view of subject and object; holding this dualistic view is a distraction. We want to leave our rigpa by itself, free from the concepts of subject and object.

The second distraction is dualistic thoughts. When we begin to meditate and focus on something, then immediately thoughts arise. We are thinking about our job, our family, America, Nepal, India, many thoughts suddenly appear in our mind. Our meditation shouldn't be deluded by those thoughts; it should be kept nakedly; our rigpa should be aware of itself without any distractions by these dualistic thoughts.

When we are relaxing our mind, the text says we should concentrate on the natural state, without self-grasping. Our mind should be free from expectations, doubts and any thoughts. We should not wonder whether something could be or not, whether we will get something or not by practicing, whether we will see some extraordinary things if we practice, or whether we will achieve some high level. Any doubts and expectations interfere with our concentration. We need to be aware and present, focusing clearly on the object of our meditation, not clouded or obscured, but focused clearly in the state of concentration. We call this a state of clarity, a state of presence. We should concentrate clearly and continue it, repeat it again and again, until we reach the level of freedom from the distractions and obstacles that we have just talked about.

People who meditate often complain that they are trying hard not to have any thoughts, trying not to generate thoughts. Some say that when they are meditating, they see some things coming to them and they wonder what they mean. "Is this a good sign that I have a feeling of strong light? Did I see a Sanggye?" Actually, these have nothing to do with a state of concentration. Thoughts and visions arise as spontaneous arisings from the state of kunzhi. In Dzogchen we talk about *lhundrub*, which means that everything is perfected in its nature and arises spontaneously. If we follow these thoughts and visions, and ask what they could mean, this distracts us from our meditation. We are not stable and not focused on what we are supposed to focus on. We are simply watching those appearances, watching where they came from and where they go.

It's important to cut those thoughts off. Following them is meaningless. We are practicing stability, zhine, trying to remain focused on our object. These appearances arise in their own way. They don't affect us, unless we chase after them. So, we should try to maintain our concentration and stay focused on our object, instead of following those appearances. If we do that, gradually we will gain stability. Appearances will continue to arise, but we should not let them distract us. This zhine practice is very important to allow us to gain stability without distractions from appearances. This is the base of our stability. Once we have achieved this stability, then we can practice anywhere, because our practice will be with us without any disturbance. That is the essence of relaxing our mind in the state of concentration.

## Discipline or Rules of Practice

The fourth point of this session is the discipline or rules of practice we should know and follow. While we are meditating and practicing this session, it's quite important, especially for beginners, not to force our meditation. We should not try to have long sessions that are unstable and full of distractions. Rather, we should do short meditation sessions, doing them often, and trying our best to be very precise in our meditation. The text advises us that, at the beginning, we should practice for the length of time needed to complete one trengwa of the SA LE Ö nyenpa. We should practice these short sessions until we will develop some stability. We should practice very precisely as the text says, and as our teacher guides us, without distractions.

Sometimes, the moment we begin to meditate, an interesting thought arises, and we get completely lost in it. Sometimes the thoughts are so nice that we start enjoying them, and we completely forget our practice and just watch them. At the end of the session, we may be happy, but we haven't achieved our goal of quality meditation. In this case, start with a short session. Set a timer if you want to. Do two or three sessions of five minutes of stable and distraction-free meditation. Then, without getting tired or hesitating, do another short session. Then, take a little break, stand up, do something else, come back, and sit again and again.

The text advises us that we should never finish our sessions in a disturbed state. We should try to end with good quality of stability and clear concentration. We should not leave in the middle of practice due to distraction, saying that we are tired. When we are distracted, we should calm down, take a deep breath, and focus again. When, after practicing again and again, we reach the moment of great concentration and stability, then we can stop meditating, and dedicate our practice.

Short sessions are the right way for beginning the practice. When we realize that we have made progress in our stability, then we should extend the length of our sessions. Sometimes, if time allows, we should practice a whole week retreat, or at least a weekend retreat. Then, we can divide one day into four practice sessions, giving us time for long sessions, when we are well-stabilized and more familiar with meditation. Between the sessions, when we take a break, it's important to practice lamé naljor, compassion practice, and refuge practice, in order to understand the essence of the teachings on a deeper level. This will help us refresh and develop our view.

The text also advises us to be careful not to engage in violent or rough actions while doing this practice. We should also watch our behavior. Some behaviors are like a skin rash; the more you scratch them, the more they itch. These behaviors can lead us to distractions, disturbances, and negativities. This applies especially to beginners, who are just entering the practice of stability. They are very sensitive, and their concentration can easily be affected. For example, it's helpful to avoid jumping, fast running, hard physical work, singing, shouting, speaking loudly etc. From our discussions about body posture, we already know that we can calm ourselves down by certain physical activities. Some activities create disturbances and imbalances in our energy, inner elements, organs, and physical structure. These disturbances and imbalances affect our mind and our concentration.

We should avoid staying close to a heat source, and not stay in direct sunshine, to avoid overheating ourselves. This can distract us. Also, avoid foods like garlic, that make us sleepier and less clear. If some particular food or beverage disturbs you, avoid it. We should also avoid alcohol, because it affects our mental clarity, so we cannot develop our practice.

The four best times for practice are: in the early morning; before noon; the evening; and at night. The middle of the day and the middle of the night are not good times for meditation, because most of us at that time are unclear, both physically and mentally. At those times, we can rest and relax, or recite prayers and nyenpas. In Tibet at that time of day, practitioners on retreats practice reciting lamé naljor, do circumambulations and prostrations in their cave, perform mandala offerings, etc.

According to Lachen Drenpa Namkha and Gongdzo Ritroed Chenpo, the beginner practitioner may experience being one hundred times happy and one hundred times unhappy. This means that our practice at the beginning is always changing. Sometimes it goes very well, and sometimes poorly. Don't let experiences, or signs of progress, or visions, or appearances inflate your ego or agitate you. Don't be disappointed when your practice has ups and downs. That is the nature of practice at the beginning. Only when we reach the state of stability will the ups and downs disappear. The main thing is to practice continuously, enthusiastically, and without disappointment.

By practicing this way, we will develop the first stage of zhine, what is referred to as "conditional zhine." This is a zhine created by our own thoughts. Then comes the second stage, referred to as "natural zhine," when we stabilize naturally. Then, we will achieve ultimate, perfect stability. At the very beginning, when we see disturbances coming, we try to be clearer and more aware, and by doing that, little by little, we will experience the zhine, and we will achieve certain stability. After a while, we won't even have to think about it or focus on it; we will simply enter the state of meditation and abide in it. The final, ultimate state of zhine can be achieved by this gradual practice. This is the very foundation of our meditation practice.

It is important to develop this state of stability, free from distractions, so we can develop our practice. The text says we should practice continually, at least ten to fifteen days, even a month, without interruption. That way we will be able to experience and stabilize our zhine.

# Integration of Internal and External Space

Now we begin the seventh session, to develop our realization. This topic is the second subdivision mentioned in the Session Six. The seventh session has three subdivisions. The first is gazing and focusing; the second is the experiences and visual projections, both inner and external, that arise as the result of practice; and the third is the introduction of our natural state of mind.

## Key Points in Gazing and Focusing

Drenpa Namkha said that a bird cannot fly unless it stretches out its wings, expends effort, and is energetic, precise, and focused. So, we must be determined, energetic, focused, and present on our practice. To achieve full enlightenment, according to the Dzogchen view, there is no other way than by realizing our true state of mind. To do that, after receiving the introduction to our natural state of mind, we have to be completely present while we are practicing. While we are gazing into external space, we must be aware of our inner space, which is the true essence of the Nature of Mind.

Gongdzo Ritro Chenpo said the essential instruction to realize our natural state is to be present, awake, energetic, and completely relaxed, and leave everything as it is, without any interference from our thoughts. When we are meditating, it's important to be completely awake in the state of meditation, no matter what we are practicing, whether it is compassion, emptiness, or the natural state of mind. In every meditation, we should be present with full energy and awareness of what we are focusing on, but without any pressure—relaxed. This is the essential point that he makes in his teachings.

According to Özer Pagmed, another great master from the past, great practitioners have great experience and realization of practice by gazing into space, with their eyes completely open, and integrating the nature of external space with the true nature of their state of mind. We should be physically disciplined. We should be awake and energetic. We should not be distracted by emotions. When visions and thoughts arise, we should not follow them. We should remain in clarity. We should realize that things are rootless. We should contemplate continuously in the non-dual state of meditation.

Those great masters who have achieved realization by that practice are known as great yogis or *naljorpas*. Özer Pagmed calls this practice "the way of snow-lion gazing." This name comes from the fact that, when we see snow lions in paintings or statutes of snow lions in front of Chinese temples, the snow lion is raising up its neck and looking straight into space.

To achieve the result, we need to concentrate our mind on the space that our eyes are focusing on. The text says that, at the same time we are gazing into the space, our rigpa (awareness) has to follow our gaze to the space we are focusing on. Our rigpa has to follow our eyes to where they focus. If we look into space, but our rigpa roams somewhere else, we will not achieve the result. The text says we also need to be present energetically and completely integrate into oneness with the space where our eyes are gazing. Our focus and rigpa cannot be separate; we must be contemplating in the oneness of them.

We should practice without attaching to external conditions and beings, without planning, and without being distracted by internal appearances. There should be no external or internal distractions. With clear presence, with the complete force of our energy, with perfect clarity, without a shadow of doubt, and rootlessly, not relying on any material support, we simply focus our rigpa on the state of oneness with space. That's it. We don't use any material support to remain in concentration. We are free from dualistic thoughts and appearances. They may appear, but they don't bother us. We completely liberate them. And we continue in that state. We extend the time of our meditation longer and longer.

The deeper we get into this state, the longer we can extend the time of meditation, remaining in this state without any distractions.

As before, it's important to avoid certain foods, drinks, and physical activities that may cause instability and imbalance to our body and health. And always, until we get certain experiences and realization of stability, it's very important to continue our practice tirelessly and enthusiastically.

## The Appearance of Results of Practice

After a certain time, we will have the inner experience that all appearances and conditions have no essence, no innate stable form, no certainty, no roots. When we practice properly, this experience naturally grows by itself. We will also see that our rigpa is awakened and relaxed in its own state, naked, without any distractions. It's present, relaxed, and comfortable, both when we practice and when we look at the material environment. Appearances continue to arise during meditation, but they do not bother us. Similarly, when we see things in the material world and experience things internally, neither the external nor internal conditions and appearances will disturb our concentration and meditation in the state of emptiness. When we have this kind of experience, it means we have gained stability, and realized and experienced how to practice the integration of internal and external space properly.

The text gives an example of an eagle flying in the sky. There are no obstacles in the sky to his flight. Once he lifts up from the ground and flies in the sky, he has no doubt whether he is flying or not. He has no fears, no doubts, and is fully confident in his journey. In the same way, we should have no fears or doubts. We should feel fully confident, with full authority in our practice. Obstacles don't matter at all. They will not disturb us; they will just appear without bothering us. Dullness, agitation, weakness, or lack of focus will not bother us once we have achieved this level of experience. By this practice we will be free from the egoism that binds us all. We will be completely free from all dualistic bonds. Moreover, the activities of the five poisons will no longer bother us. We will overcome all inner and outer obstacles. The text says that this is the base of progress of our practice and the development of our inner realization; this is a foundation of our knowledge, a method of following and progressing on the path to enlightenment. This is the essential method, and we should realize it.

## The Introduction of the Natural State

The third part of this session introduces external gazing and internal qualities, using the example of the space of the sky and the space of our natural state. In the second part, we talked about gazing into empty space; while we are focusing on the empty space, our awareness, rigpa, has to follow our eyes to the space where our eyes are focusing.

Now the text explains how the example of the empty space of the sky applies to qualities of our Nature of Mind.

The space inside a house is not different from the space outside the house. The nature of the space inside the house and the space outside the house is not different. We are the ones that create the difference, saying "this is inner space and that is outer space." We make the boundary with our dualistic thoughts, because of a wall standing there. If the wall falls down, we can't distinguish internal space from external space. All the space is equally empty.

To practice this, we should go to a place without much wind and with a wide view over an empty space. (We choose a place without wind because we practice with open eyes, and wind would bother our eyes.) Sit in the five-point body posture, as usual. Gaze into external space. On the physical level, we say our eyes are looking into space. It seems that we are looking at external emptiness. But the barrier between the external emptiness and the internal emptiness is created by our thoughts. We think, "I'm looking outwards." In reality, there is no separation, no difference between the emptiness of the physical space that we are looking into, and the emptiness of our true Nature of Mind. The space of both of them has the same quality of emptiness. We only need to overcome the limited, incorrect view created by our dualistic thoughts. The nature of the inner space is inseparable from the nature of the outer space. Our rigpa has to go into the external space and completely integrate with it, into oneness. Once we begin to realize that, once we enter that oneness, then we have integrated into the true space of our own nature.

Another example is when we set out nine bowls of different shapes and fill them with water. The moon will reflect in the water with nine different shapes, according to the shape of the bowl. But in reality, the moon has only one essence. We see nine different moons in nine different shapes, because our eyes see the containers and their shapes. But if we pour all the water into one large bowl, we will see only one reflection of the moon, not nine. These different shapes are similar to our inner reflections. We say that one container is round, another has a different shape, and we give them names and titles and turn them into what we perceive them to be. But in essence, there is only one moon, one essence of the moon. We must realize that our illusion tells us there are nine reflections of the moon in nine different shaped bowls; but in reality, they all have the same essence. We integrate ourselves into the real essence of oneness, to integrate the internal and external space.

Naturally, we have a concept of self, of "I," "me," and "mine." Our mind is very powerful, very alert within us, and it is protecting our self. Here, when we are talking about our mind, our "I," we are talking about its nature, its essence. If we search carefully for our mind, we can't find its color, size, shape, source, where it comes from and where it goes, how it comes and goes. We can realize a state, which is the same as the empty space outside; but still we experience the presence of our mind in that space, very active, energetic, and clear, even though we cannot identify it or find its shape or color. This shows that the Nature of Mind is empty.

## Pe Dön Tak Sum and the Example of the Sky

An important concept in Dzogchen is "example, essence, and reason," or *pe dön tak sum*. *Pe* means "example;" *dön* means "essence" or "reality;" and *tak* means "reason." We use the example, (*pe*) of the sky. The essence (*dön*) of the sky is emptiness. For this reason (*tak*), the nature of our mind is also emptiness.

The text says that the fortunate students are introduced to meditate on oneness, on the equal state of internal and external essence. Students receive introduction by the example of the external sky that we can see. It has no color, no shape, no beginning, no end, and no sides. It's equal in all directions; it's the same empty space. And there is nothing we can identify as this empty space. We can simply experience it, integrate with it, fly into it, but this space in itself has no form, no direction, no colors; we cannot measure it. It's simply vast empty space that is empty, formless, and rootless. There is no form, no root, nothing inherently existing or objective. The essence and meaning of the sky is the same as our natural state of mind.

When we are gazing into space, we are not able to find or identify anything in this space. Similarly, although our mind is actively present and active, generating good and bad thoughts, we cannot prove that our mind exists as something solid. There is no shape, no form, no size, no source. This indicates that the true nature of the mind is completely empty as the space. We have to integrate these two and realize that the Nature of Mind is as empty as the sky.

This doesn't mean it doesn't exist. It exists in the empty state, within the vastness of space. But it has no form. It's not an object we can identify. It's not enough to know it's empty; we have to realize and experience that emptiness. We all know, without doubt, that the space in front of us has no shape, color, etc. It's the same with our mind, only we don't realize it. Here we are trying to explain the way our mind is, and when we understand that, to realize it. This understanding has to be practiced again and again, until it becomes an inner realization of the true Nature of Mind, of emptiness, of the quality of emptiness.

The text gives us the example: the sign and its meaning. We have to integrate them into oneness. That is the purpose of gazing into the sky. Without this purpose, we would just gaze into the sky like a madman. It wouldn't make any sense. By gazing into space, we should realize that the essence of the space we are gazing into, and the essence of our internal space, our mind's nature, is the same nature. We have to integrate them into oneness. When we are able to do that, we are integrating the essence of the meaning of the sign we were given through the example.

When, after some practice, we are able to remain in the contemplation of that realization as long as possible without any obstacles, we call it contemplation in the nature of *bönku*, primordial state, the nature of Bön. That is how we must practice until we get a clear realization. Once we achieve this realization, we can apply it to all existing phenomena, not just our mind and space, but all internal and external phenomena. We start with the example of external and internal space, because it is easier to understand. But once we have realized this, we can change the object of our contemplation to anything we like.

The text says that the nature of our mind is not limited to these given examples, signs, and their meaning. These examples are simply given to lead practitioners to a realization of their natural state of mind. We should not limit ourselves to these examples. Normally, the Dzogchen teachings tell us simply to relax and stay in the contemplation of the natural state of mind. But for the beginners, this is not easy; it's hard to do this if you have no idea what it means. The purpose of these examples is to lead us towards realization.

When we practice, it's good to practice continually for nine, ten, eleven, or fifteen days, until we get a sense of realization. This practice gives us not only stability, zhine, but also realization, *lhagthong*, which is wisdom, awareness. Gaining stability and simultaneously achieving realization of the true quality of our mind is an essential part of the progress of our practice.

# Introduction of the Nature of Mind through Visualization and Breath

This is the eighth session. This session begins with a prostration to our root teacher.

The eighth session introduces the natural state of mind. The eighth session has three parts: (a) introducing the *kunzhi jang chub kyi sem*, the *zhi rang jung yeshe*, the base of all, the natural state; (b) clearing the stains and negativities of dualistic thoughts; and (c) following the path of wisdom.

## Introducing the Natural State

The first part of this session concerns introducing the natural state. This first part is divided into two parts: (i) how to meditate properly, and (ii) how to introduce the natural state.

### (i) How to Meditate Properly.

The Dzogchen text, *Drang Dön,* says:

> *In the secret level, tsa, lung, and thigle,*
>
> *Meditating on rigpa, the mind is the supreme refuge.*

Lachen Drenpa Namka says:

> *Your body itself is like a crystal tube.*
>
> *Visualize three channels, like a crystal palace of light.*
>
> *Expel the inner wind out, like shooting an arrow.*
>
> *Bring the outer wind in, like drawing a bow.*
>
> *Move the middle wind that was being held.*
>
> *This will achieve the qualities of meditation.*

According to various Dzogchen texts and teachers, we should sit in the five-point meditation posture. We should visualize the three channels, as when we practice the nine-fold breathing practice. The right channel is white, the left channel is red, and the central channel is blue. In some practices, women visualize the red and white channels on the opposite sides. In some practices, the central channel is much bigger than the other two; in this practice, the central channel is the same size as the red and white channels. The central channel starts at the junction of the other two channels at the level of the secret chakra and goes up along the spine to the crown chakra level, opening up like a long trumpet. Normally we visualize that the two side channels bend under the skull and open at the nostrils, but in this practice, we see them open at the top of our head, at the sides of the central channel.

Above the crown chakra we should visualize the Tibetan syllables A and MA, which symbolize yab (male) and yum (female). Visualize the A on the right side and the MA on the left. These syllables transform into *thigles* (drops of light), the A into a white thigle, and the MA into a red thigle, each the size of a pea.

Then, we take three normal breaths, thinking that we are cleansing all the negativities of past, present, and future, all sicknesses of bile, mucus, and wind, and all obstacles created by male, female, and *naga* spirits. We are cleansing all the negativities and emotions cultivated in the past, present, and future; we are cleaning our body. During these three breaths, the thigles remain at the sides of the crown.

Then we inhale slowly, normally. Hold the breath and tighten the lower organs. While we hold our breath, the thigles above us enter the right and left channels, and come down to the junction of the channels. We should hold our breath as long as we can, with a clear vision of the movement of the thigles. When the thigles enter the central channel, we can visualize them either as going one above the other, or as dissolving into one. Then we imagine the thigles coming up the central channel, coming out, separating again into two, and staying at both sides of the crown of your head. When we cannot hold our breath any more, take a short breath, not a long one, and repeat the cycle, again holding the breath. We should visualize five, seven, nine, ten, fifteen, or twenty-one cycles. When we really cannot hold our breath any longer, start the cycle again, and instead of sending the two thigles up to the opening of the central channel, they combine into one and go up the central channel to the heart level. When they get there, we dissolve them by saying the syllable HA or PHAT, forcefully, from the inside, not just from the lips. We visualize that the combined thigle disappears into empty space. We then remain in the state of dissolution of that thigle, in the natural state of mind.

When we hold our breath, we hold it carefully, without too much pressure, but holding it down. Sometimes, if we swallow, it helps to bring the breath down. Hold the breath and visualization while the thigle is at the heart level, before dissolving it. If we say "PHAT" too fast, it's not helpful. We should contemplate the state of unification and remain in it as long as we can. Don't start a new cycle too quickly. The whole point of doing this visualization is to get to that state and contemplate it.

The text says we should practice this way for five or ten days, or until we get signs of experience. The best time for this practice is in the early morning, before it's too warm, before the sun gets too hot, and also late in the evening and at night.

This particular method is very helpful for our development, but it can be also destructive if we don't do it correctly. The text says that when we have some difficulties in the practice and we feel something is not going correctly, we must get clarification from a teacher. It's also good to apply *trul khor* (a type of Tibetan yoga) practices when necessary to correct some of physical and mental imbalances.

Our A-tri text quotes from a Zhangzhung Nyengyud text, that says by doing this practice of breath, visualization, PHAT syllable, and contemplation of the natural state, we will distinguish the natural state from the dualistic appearances that arise in our contemplation, without any mixing, without influence from these dualistic appearances. It will be like lifting the cloth that covers our physical body; we will have a chance to experience the true state of mind and its qualities, nakedly and directly. We will have an experience similar to seeing the sun shining between thick clouds; meaning, in that moment we will nakedly see the natural state of mind.

When we achieve this level of realization, it's important not to obscure it by dualistic thoughts, and not try to force our own understanding or our definitions on that experience. We should remain in the state of meditation with sharp, energetic focus, without any activity of the five senses, and with no attachment to this experience. Spontaneously, automatically, the experience of joy, light, calmness, and happiness appears in that state. It's like a mute person tasting something sweet. They experience the sweet taste, but they cannot explain it. All these experiences are beyond our ability to describe and explain. We can experience it, this state is energetically present, but it's beyond our ability to explain or describe. It is called the self-born awareness. With it is the core of the heart essence of the Enlightened Ones, the ultimate essence of the Sanggye.

## (ii) Introducing the Natural State of Mind

Once there was an elder practitioner in Dolanji, who is now deceased. In our tradition, when we receive an introduction to the Nature of Mind, we should practice it for some time and then come back to our teacher and report to him what our experiences are, and what we found. Since these experiences are secret, nobody accompanies us during the conversation. When this practitioner came to report his experience to his teacher, all he could say was, "Rinpoche, I don't know how to explain this, but I do know what I experienced." The teacher asked him what his experience was, but he could only say, "I don't know how to explain this, Rinpoche, but I do know what I experienced."

When teachers introduce us to the natural state of mind, they do this based on the texts and on their own experience. They use stories, blessings, or other ways to introduce the natural state. But we have to discover the natural state ourselves, by our own practice. No one can give you the direct experience of it. The Dzogchen nature, the natural state of mind, is beyond words, names, and explanations. We have to experience and realize it individually. The teacher, through his explanations, can lead us in that direction. We can always point in some direction and say that if someone goes there, he will cross the river and come up to the mountain, and if he will follow the path, he will eventually reach the cave where he can meditate. Or, parents can point out the moon to their children, showing them that this bright, round thing is the moon. Their finger doesn't touch the moon, but it leads the children to see the real moon shining in the sky. In the same way, although the natural state is beyond names, descriptions, and words, we can reach it. The teacher can lead us to it, if we are able to follow the instructions the teacher gives us and put in our effort and time.

Other Dzogchen texts and masters advise us to just look into our Nature of Mind. It's called the nature, but there is nothing we can see. It is what it is. It means that we will not see anything through great effort and expectations, or by creating our own ideas of what the natural state will look like. If we try to see it this way, we will not see anything. We can only see it the way it is. And when I talk about seeing it, I don't mean seeing with our eyes, but realizing it through rigpa. We can understand it, integrate it, and unite our rigpa into oneness with this true state of the Nature of Mind. We cannot even say that rigpa is seeing the natural state of mind. There are not two things, no subject or object. Rigpa and the natural state are integrated into one in the experience of our practice.

If you have practiced zhine using the support of an A syllable, normally we practice this continually for one week, six sessions a day. There are certain moments in our practice when we do it right; we feel we completely dissolve into the A; sometimes we feel that both we and the object are diminishing into the space, and that only emptiness remains. That sense of oneness, without any material object, is part of the training to focus more precisely on our object. The real essence is not relying on support from the object. That is just a method, like a finger pointing to the moon, to enter our nature in a more stable and precise way without any interference from the arising of busy thoughts. In that short moment of experience, we are in the state of oneness with the space of nature. If any of you had this experience in the practice of zhine, this is a good example.

Lishu Tagring, the great Bönpo *rigdzin* and scholar, said: "This is it! Why do we say that we don't know it? This is what it is." When a great master explains to us that "This is it," and asks why it is so hard for us to realize it, it is because he has achieved the realization nakedly, directly. When the master points to something and says, "This is it," it's almost as if he were showing us some object standing in front of us. It means that this state is just there, within us. Our mind hasn't been separated from us; it is with us in every moment. And if our mind hasn't been separated from us, the nature of our mind also has never been separated from us. It is with us in each and every moment. That means it is not coming from outside or inside; it's there in its own place. It's about the way we look at ourselves. Without making it complicated, the master advises us to just be simple, relax, and look into our own nature. This is what he means. Just look at the mind itself and then we will realize its nature. It's easy to say, but when we try to meditate, it's different.

According to a text called *Bhum*, our rigpa (the *rang rig yeshe*) does not appear from outside or inside. It's there, in its own place. That is the meaning of Lishu Tagring's words, when he says, "That is it! Why is it so complicated to realize it? Why do we complain we cannot realize it?" The dho text says that we shouldn't waste efforts to find anything outside of us, or to search inside. None of this is required. Simply by relaxing within ourselves we will find our nature; it's there. That is the point of this quotation. This is a method of progressing and developing our realization faster. This way, we can nakedly realize our Nature of Mind—realize it as a mother and child uniting in oneness in the empty space of awareness of rigpa itself.

One of the early Bönpo masters had practiced and developed the stability of zhine, so he could abide in meditation for a long period of time. He had stability, but with confusion, without clarity, and without sharpness. He could stay in a calm state, feeling some joy; he could stay that way without physical or mental difficulty; but this wasn't the realization of the Nature of Mind. Once he went to a Zhang Zhung master and reported his practices to him. The master said that his practice was just stability, and his focus on the Nature of Mind was not sharp enough. It was just simple zhine, not completely dull, but not real calm abiding in the nature. The master advised him to practice the method of breathing and visualization we have just described, to increase his clarity and focus. He did as the master advised him, and after some time, achieved great results of his practice.

This story tells us this particular method of breathing and visualization helps us to develop our practice and clears confusion and lack of stability. It gives us both stability and realization, with a clear understanding of our own nature. That is the purpose and benefit of this eighth session and of this practice.

The text also tells us that, while there are many practices we may do to achieve the realization of the Nature of Mind, this particular breathing and visualization practice, more than anything else, will lead us to realization. The text says, "My dear sons, practice this method, and very soon it will lead you to the state you expect to achieve." The text also says to practice this method from ten to fifteen days. This doesn't guarantee that if you will practice for ten to fifteen days you will surely achieve realization. It simply means we should do the practice continuously, instead of doing it for one day, then leaving it for a week or two, then again doing it for a day. We should do the practice for some time, at least to get used to it physically, then to get familiar with the visualization, and then on the inner level of concentration. If we do all this very precisely and with great effort, continuously for ten to fifteen days, even if we don't achieve complete realization, it will lead our practice in the right way and we will gain more results. When we practice in the right way, it only requires effort and enthusiasm to continue and improve it.

If we practice for a short while, we may have a good experience and feel joy. If we stop practicing because of our busy schedule, and then return to practice after a week or so, we may not even feel the joy again. Once we have that kind of experience, we should continue to practice, with no attachment and no expectations, thinking that we are continuing on the path of practice as the teachings describe it. If we do this, then we will achieve results.

When we begin, it's difficult to settle our physical body for even five minutes without pain. And our inner self is so busy, so wild, it takes time to settle everything and bring it back to normal. We have to settle our inner energy, mainly our wind energy, and calm our inside by abiding in stable concentration without distraction. Then, as our practice progresses, there are moments when we achieve the first signs of realization. These signs become more frequent and grow stronger as we improve our realization—our real, naked realization—unification of mother and son, the natural state of mind and rigpa. All teachings are talking about these same two things: the natural state and our rigpa should realize each other and integrate into oneness.

# Meditation on the Natural State of Mind

This is the ninth of the fifteen sessions, which talks about meditation on the natural state of mind.

There are three main parts: (a) how to remain with stability in the natural state; (b) how to awaken and refresh our meditation, overcoming the manifestations arising from their base, and (c) the continuation of meditation in the natural state of mind into the activities of our day-to-day life.

## Remaining in the Natural State of Mind

A Dzogchen text says that remaining in the natural state of mind has the nature of joy. When we remain in the Nature of Mind, we are on the pathway of meditation.

According to Tonpa Shenrab:

> *"Leave your state of mind clear, without grasping thought. Leave the five doors (five senses) free (meaning, don't grasp at sensory experiences). Leave pervasive rigpa as it is. Leave both body and mind unmodified and relaxed."*

Lachen Drenpa Namka said:

> *"Whatever appearances arise, they are self-arising. Do not attach to them. Leave them freely and openly. Meditate without distraction. Unify both subject and object as inseparable."*

Gongdzo Ritro Chenpo tells us we should leave everything in its own way, relaxing openly and flexibly, without modifying anything. He is saying that the kunzhi (the base, or the mother) and rigpa (the awareness, or the son) should remain in that state without interference from spontaneously arising appearances.

160

As we have discussed, in Dzogchen we refer to kunzhi as the mother and rigpa as the son. The essence of kunzhi is empty; its nature is clarity and luminous light; and its manifestation is *tsal*, spontaneous arising. When we are within the natural state of mind, appearances often come, spontaneously self-arising in their own state. We should just leave them as they are, without any effort, without any attempt to remove the thought, just leave everything as it is.

The *tsal*, or manifestation aspect of the natural state, has no limits and no conditions. When we meditate, appearances arise spontaneously. We cannot prevent this. But if we chase after these appearances, we lose our focus and become deluded by dualistic thoughts. We cannot stop this process by expending effort or with dualistic thoughts. For this reason, we leave it in its own state. When we are able to focus in our natural state of mind, without any interferences or disturbance from appearances, we call it meditating in the natural state of mind.

How do we identify our natural state of mind? This is the key point. Of course, it's important to get an introduction from our teacher on what the natural state is, and to make sure we understand it clearly and focus on it correctly.

Different practitioners have different experiences and different explanations. Very often, scholars from other traditions say that in Dzogchen, both in Nyingma and Bön schools, there is nothing to meditate, because the masters say to leave everything, without thinking, and just meditate on the natural state of mind.

Sometimes, teachers tell students to just sit and think about nothing. If we analyze this carefully, we see that we are still thinking about something. On the one hand, there is a thought that we must not think about anything else. On the other hand, when we experience self-arising appearances, we think that we shouldn't be thinking about them, because they are just self-arising. Our concentration is focused on the appearances, not the natural state. We are focused on the wrong thing.

Some people make a great effort to stop thoughts from arising. Others remain in the state with no clear focus. Practitioners have to be careful not to do these things.

Our meditation begins with a concept, an intention to meditate on the natural state of mind. When we begin to meditate, some experiences arise, and we should leave them alone, without chasing or grasping, without modifying them by our thought, without thinking that the natural state should be this way or that way. We may compare the natural state of mind to the state we experience when we work very hard or carry something heavy, and then suddenly we release it. We are left with no thought of doing any other activity.

If we begin to search for our Nature of Mind, we will lose everything. If we try to see it by force, through the activity of our dualistic thought, we will see nothing. If we force ourselves to meditate by thinking "I am meditating on the natural state of mind," with a concept or attitude that our meditation is bound in the natural state of mind, it will also cause the true state of focus to disappear. Therefore, Gongdzo Ritro Chenpo says, if we do too much, or if we are too active, we are in danger of losing the path to enlightenment and coming back to the same state of cyclic existence.

When we say we will leave everything in its nature, without doing anything, this seems simple. But it is the most difficult thing to do. We may have a brief experience of being in the natural state of mind, but sometimes we don't realize it clearly, and sometimes we don't have enough strength to remain in this state without letting this experience disappear.

We may experience being in the natural state of mind for a short time, but then we lose the state. We may experience certain self-arising appearances. These appearances only disturb us when we lose our focus and begin to chase after them. When this happens, it's important to put more effort into our focus and presence. If we get confused, we should ask our teacher for clarification and keep contact with our teacher by praying, practicing lamé naljor, and doing other practices to receive blessings.

When we meditate on the natural state of mind, we need to be aware, awakened, present, and conscious. Our focus has to be very sharp. That strength of focus will protect us from the interference of appearances. Often, at the beginning of our meditation session, our focus is clear and sharp, and so is our awareness; but gradually, because of a lack of sharp focus and weakness of our awareness, our protection from interferences weakens.

# How to Awaken and Refresh Our Meditation While Remaining in the Natural State

When we meditate on the Nature of Mind, we have to overcome the appearances of thoughts or other interferences, and we have to overcome them without letting them interfere with our focus. We have to overcome both the concept of meditation on the natural state of mind, and the concept of non-meditation on the natural state of mind. According to one of the ngags, we will not be able to find the Enlightened One by meditating; we should rather let self-arising rigpa arise. We will not recognize the arising rigpa, we should rather leave it clearly, with sharp focus of our meditation. This means we cannot meditate by force and concepts. Our ordinary thoughts will delude us. Dualistic thoughts cannot discover, identify, or stabilize the natural state of mind. We may only discover the natural state of mind by just leaving it within its own state.

The text says that, "remaining in the state of meditation without a dualistic view, we should meditate without meditating." This quotation makes two important points. First, "meditating without meditating" means we must free ourselves from the concept of meditation on the natural state of mind. Second, we must remain in meditation without a dualistic view. This means we should be in meditation with presence, awake, with clear, sharp focus and energy, but without dualistic thoughts.

Lhachen Drenpa Namkha said we should release completely, like we were taking a heavy load off our back. We should be completely relaxed, aware and present. We should be completely free and flexible, which means that we should have no concept of tension or chasing the arising thoughts.

We may meditate with closed eyes, but our mind may still be chasing arising thoughts, one after another. Instead of focusing on the natural state of mind, we are focusing on the arising appearances. Zhine can help us gain stability in our meditation.

Even if we gain stability, if we are not present, clear, and focused, then there is a good chance that obstacles will arise. We may possibly get dull, which is lack of focus and energy in our meditation. We may get wild inside. Our focus may weaken.

It is very important for practitioners to be able to distinguish between stability and the natural state of mind. When we develop a certain level of stability of zhine, we may experience certain states, like extraordinary joy, that we don't experience normally in our daily life. We may have strength to remain in that concentration as long as we want. We may also experience mental and physical joy. Experiencing these things, a practitioner may think that they are reaching the goal. However, they are not reaching the goal, but rather getting lost in the middle of the journey. We have to be aware of those things and distinguish different experiences. Zhine is good and necessary until we gain stability of concentration. On higher levels of zhine, our body feels the joy of remaining in meditation posture, our mind doesn't get tired, and we get attached to remaining in the state of concentration. We don't need to eat or drink, and we remain in that state without any difficulty. By well-developed zhine, we may also gain experience of some unusual, miraculous powers. But these experiences don't mean that we have achieved the realization of the natural state of mind; it just means we have good stability of focus.

That stability alone will not give us much benefit. If we are satisfied with our stability only, and remain in the joy of zhine, then the main purpose of our practice has escaped us. Like travelers sleeping on the road in the middle of their journey, we are not getting to our goal. In this tradition, we only use zhine as a road. Our goal is not to be on the road, but rather to reach our destination. We have to use our stability to continue our meditation on the natural state of mind. Only then will that stability be purposeful.

## Continuing the Natural State After Meditation

The third section of this session is concerned with continuing the strength of our realization of the natural state of mind after we cease that meditation. Lhachen Drenpa Namkha said that when we achieve the realization of the natural state of mind, then it is important to remain in that state. We don't necessarily have to meditate sitting cross-legged. We may keep the experience and the presence of being in the natural state while talking, walking, or sleeping, always with inner awakening and always with awareness of the natural state of mind.

As an example, if we lose something of value, the moment we learn about this loss, we are surprised and upset. After some time passes, the feeling of loss still remains, but we continue to do all our day-to-day activities with this feeling. Another way to say it is that we are always mindful, always aware of the natural state of mind. We can talk, sleep, walk, do all our daily activities, and remain in the natural state of mind.

When we speak of the great, highly realized masters, it doesn't mean they have realized something special or new. Instead, their realization has deepened, become grounded, and has been confirmed. The quality of realization is no different, because the natural state has one quality; but the level of realization differs because of their experience. Continuously remaining in the natural state of mind allows us to achieve a higher level of knowledge.

As we discussed, this session focusses on three aspects of meditation: (i) remaining in the natural state of mind; (ii) awakening and refreshing our meditation; and (iii) continuing in the natural state after mediation. How do we develop these three aspects of meditation? As usual, we meditate in the five-point meditation position, and we leave our focus without any modifications on the natural state of mind. During our meditation on the natural state of mind, we must be mindfully present with full awareness.

From time to time, between meditation sessions, we go back to the source and look for who is meditating, who is watching, who is realizing this natural state of mind? There is no subject and object, but we talk about rigpa realizing kunzhi. How do we identify the one that is realizing and the one that is being realized? It is as if both subject and object were existing there. When we look like this, the one who watches and that which is being watched will disappear. What will we realize by that? What will we gain by that search? We will realize there is no one who is meditating and no object of meditation; we will realize the unification of mother and son, of kunzhi, the true Nature of Mind, and rigpa, the awareness.

At the beginning, it's important to make the first and third phase longer. If we have only a little experience and it is unstable, then we shouldn't take the gradual steps we have just described. Instead, it is more important to remain in the natural state of mind as long as we can.

These are the first two phases of meditation: remaining in the natural state of mind and refreshing our meditation. We should develop these two phases of meditation so we experience stability and clarity, and so we can be confident that we are properly meditating on the natural state of mind. The third phase, continuing in the natural state, must be focused, lively and energetic, not dull and vague.

At the end of our development stage, when we are advanced, the continuation practice is the most important. When we are at a highly-developed level, with full authority and understanding of the true nature of all phenomena, then in every moment of our day-to-day life activities, in all the six periods of the day, for the full twenty-four hours, we can be aware of our realization.

At this advanced level, we are completely overruling our normal way of meditation. In our normal meditation, we go through a process to reach the natural state. At the higher level, when we are in continuous awareness, we don't need any special effort or guidance. The moment we think of the natural state of mind, we are in it; the moment we think we need to release and refresh our meditation, we just do it.

In early times the great masters performed miracles within the state of the Nature of Mind. They manifested blessings, manifested themselves in many forms, so they could be seen in two or three places at one time, they left handprints in stones, and so on. They could do all this while they were within the realization of the Nature of Mind beyond conditions. If we are developing these experiences, then every moment of our life is connected with practice. As the text says, we don't need a special place for meditation. At a high level of realization, we don't depend on the place we are meditating in. We can meditate in a crowd, on the train, in a bus station, or in a completely isolated cave. We are no longer bound, because we have realized the true state, the true nature not only of our mind, but of all phenomena. And if we go back to the true nature of all phenomena, where we are makes no difference; the nature of phenomena is the same everywhere.

We read in biographies that great Dzogchen masters sometimes appear to be childish. They are beyond doubts and expectations. For a Dzogchen yogi who is absolutely beyond all conditions and dualistic thoughts, it doesn't matter if you praise him or insult him with harsh words. It makes no difference if you dress nicely or wear worn clothes. Material conditions don't matter for him. Ordinary people see such yogis as crazy and mad, but they are filled with wisdom, and the perceptions of others don't make any difference to them.

Students who receive one or two lessons from such masters cannot develop their inner wisdom very quickly. It is difficult and takes time. But some students are like puppies trying to be snow lions. They want to pretend they are Dzogchen masters. They do funny things; they dress strangely and act strangely in public, declaring they don't care about anything. And if someone tells them they shouldn't behave like that, they quote some Dzogchen text and say that nothing matters. That is behaving like a puppy pretending to be a snow lion. We must not behave that way. Once we fully realize the natural state, we will be beyond conditions. But until then, living in society, we have to take social norms into account, or else we will cultivate negative karma.

# Integration of Body, Speech, and Mind

This is the tenth session. This session teaches us to put our stainless awareness into the Path of Practice. This session has four subdivisions: practice by body, practice by speech, practice by mind, and practice by strong emotions. When we practice in the natural state of mind, we shall remain in the state of continuation of meditation in our day-to-day activities and integrate the practice into our daily life. In this way, any positive experience we gain through our daily practice becomes part of our life.

# How To Integrate Our Practice into Daily Life

## Body

First, while we remain in the state of realization of our true Nature of Mind, we can check and experiment by moving our body, to see if we can remain in the natural state while moving. At the very beginning, we can touch our body, rub it, move it slightly, and check how much we can continue our practice of contemplation in the natural state of mind. We improve slowly, step by step, until we get used to doing these movements and can do them without affecting our meditation and focus on the natural state of mind. When we get used to it and we can do it without disturbing our concentration, then we can stand up, and walk a bit in a smooth, peaceful manner. Again, we check whether we can remain in the natural state of mind while we are walking or not.

Gradually we may increase our motion, walk faster, and do different activities. If we can perform these activities while maintaining our presence in the natural state, then we can do more physical activities, such as prostrations, while continuing in the natural state. In this way, we are expanding the time and activity level of our practice. If we are able to do those movements without disturbing our practice, it means all our day-to-day life can be carried out within the state of practice. We can practice while doing our day-to-day activities and tending to our daily business. We don't waste a single moment. All our daily activities can be transformed into practice. In this way, we become free from grasping (*zin me*).

## Speech

When we can perform body movements in the natural state, we then move to speech. We recite prayers and chant nyenpas, and check how much we can do without getting distracted from being in the natural state. If we are stable, then we can develop this aspect by doing different ceremonies and rituals, then having general conversations, then singing, and so on. We do this slowly, step by step, according to our ability. When we are stable in the natural state while performing these speech activities, it means our speech aspect is connecting to our practice. We can activate our speech while remaining in practice. In this way, we are fully aware of the discovery of the natural state.

## Mind

The third aspect is our mind, our thoughts. To begin, while remaining in the natural state, we can imagine we transform ourselves into a deity, a protector, either peaceful or wrathful. It is similar to the integration of body and speech we have discussed already. Gradually, when we can do this all without any problems, then we can imagine different thoughts. We can think all that we wish, and so long as the thoughts don't disturb our practice, we experience all those activities as a part of our practice. We can even experiment by generating the five poisons to see if we can maintain the natural state while thinking about them. If we are able to integrate all these activities into our practice, it means that we can transform all actions of our mind into practice. We can transform them into virtuous deeds.

## Strong Emotions

The fourth exercise the text mentions is to imagine some frightening experience, some joyful moment, and all sorts of things that we experience in day-to-day life—pleasant and unpleasant, happy and sorrowful, good and bad, suffering and happiness—while remaining in the natural state. We can think of the wars and conflicts in the world. We can imagine the death of a person we are close to and feel how much that would hurt us. All this time, we remain in the natural state, without being affected by these experiences.

Continuation of practice doesn't mean that we are supposed to sit in meditation and do all these things. Instead we should perform the activities of body, speech, and mind while continuing to remain in the full awareness of our Nature of Mind. If we are able to do this, then each moment of our daily life is transformed into practice, and every deed we perform is connected to our practice. According to one of the Dzogchen texts, when we can remain in the natural state and perform all these activities without our natural state being influenced, then we may be called Dzogchen practitioners.

What's most important in this practice is that we should do all our activities in the presence of being in the natural state. Without making any distinctions, without allowing or not allowing, accepting or not accepting certain actions based on conditions, we should realize everything as a spontaneous manifestation.

The text tells us that we should develop this practice gradually, step by step, through body, speech, and mind, as we have described earlier. First, we develop them one by one. When we become more familiar with the practice, we can do two and three together. In the beginning, it's very distracting to incorporate body, speech, and mind. Gradually, as we continue this practice, we will reach a point where, instead of distractions and disturbances, we will feel it as a path. All actions will appear in their own way. Without any special preparation, we will see that we are doing meditation or prostrations while remaining in the natural state of mind. Without creating the thought or intention, we naturally enter such action with awareness of our natural state of mind, without discriminating, avoiding, or rejecting any situation or thing. When we have that experience, then all the events will support the development of our practice. At that time, all our actions will be within the state of continuation of the meditation on the natural state of mind.

We also say that, if we remain in contemplation of the natural state of mind before going to bed and falling asleep, or we keep the visualization of our teacher or Shenlha Ökar—if we are able to sleep with the continuation of any of those practices—then the whole period of our sleep is a time of practice. While we are totally asleep, snoring loudly, we don't have any intention of practice at that time, but when we have begun our sleep with that intention, its strength continues into the sleep. That's why our night is not wasted. It's a period of practice. Similarly, when we realize the natural state of mind, we remain within the continuation of this state while performing various activities. Then, our daily actions are within the state of practice; this is the meaning of these teachings.

Another Dzogchen text says that we are in the natural state of mind when we realize virtuous deeds and non-virtuous deeds without the subject-object view we usually have; rather we see the oneness of subject and object. The natural state and its qualities is beyond explanations, names, conditions, and causes. It's completely beyond everything; therefore, it's perfect— spontaneously perfect. We try to stay in the natural state, beyond the distinction of subject and object.

Another Dzogchen text says that beginners shouldn't hurry into these activities until they get confirmation they are in the natural state of mind and have developed stability of their meditation. These instructions show us the method, the path to follow; but we must proceed gradually, knowing what to do when. Beginners, until they get good stability of their realization, shouldn't hurry and jump to advanced practices. It would be like a child trying to run before it can walk. Beginners must focus on achieving realization and stabilizing it.

But the text advises us that, once we achieve the natural state of mind, we should do these practices. Small streams are in danger of drying out when it gets really hot. Although there is water in them, when the water is not protected and used, it can dry out when a sudden heat comes. Similarly, once we have that realization and stability, if we don't integrate them with our daily life, it will be like not using the stream. This way, our realization is practically transformed into the path to enlightenment. If we realize something, and we don't use it practically in our life, it's useless. Imagine we were sick and had some valuable medicine that would cure us, but we wouldn't use it for its purpose. When we have some level of realization, we should use it to follow the path. No one has ever achieved enlightenment without following the path leading to it. Therefore, it's important to turn our realization into practice. Continuously remaining in our practice is our pathway.

# PART 3

# Achieving Liberation as the Result of Practice

# Practice During the Night

With the eleventh session, we begin the third main part of these teachings. The first part is the ngondro, the preliminary practices, to tame our wild mind and raise our inner awareness. The second part is the ngozhi, the actual practice, to deepen our inner practice on the path. The third part is *je kyi chawa*, to achieve liberation as the accomplishment of our practice.

This third part, *je kyi chewa*, has four major categories. The first category concerns practices done in the evening and at night. These practices include: (i) training our mind to make sleep more meaningful by contemplating the natural state of mind; (ii) developing the ability to realize when we are dreaming; (iii) realizing the dream as a dream; (iv) realize the non-solid, non-real nature of dreams, so that we do not attach to them; and (v) realize that, because the dreams are non-solid, we can transform them with our mind.

The second category concerns practice of visual experiences both at night and in the daytime, without chasing after the appearances caused by dualistic thoughts. The main focus is the realization of the quality of the dream, the realization of the dream as a dream, and the power of the dream.

The third category is to "practice to discover the flexible quality of the dream, so that we can transform and expand in any way we want."

The fourth category is contemplating and remaining in rigpa, awareness.

This first category is covered in this eleventh session, and categories two through four are covered in the subsequent sessions.

## Dreams

To begin with, it is helpful to understand what a dream is. Our dreams are projections of our own mind. Ordinary people have dreams that are based on emotions and illusions, sometimes called "karmic dreams." They perceive dreams as having some kind of solid existence, and grasp at them. In reality, dreams have no substance, no inherent existence. They are just projections of our mind, our thought. When we realize that, we can recognize that our dream is a dream, and develop it to experience the "clear light dream."

# Practice at Night

Concerning practice at night, the first point is how to practice the natural state, how to remain in it by realizing it, how to integrate it, and how to expand our realization. At first, as usual, we sit comfortably in the five-point meditation position. We can also lie down in bed, with the pillow a little higher than usual, so our torso is higher than when sleeping normally. We imagine that we are sleeping like a Sanggye. If it's possible, we should lie on our right side, with our face to the east and our head to the south. We imagine we are on a throne lifted up by a snow lion, a horse, a dragon, and a garuda, and on top of the throne are the sun and moon cushions. The lama or yidam we have connection with, or are practicing with, is sitting on that throne.

We generate the mind of compassion, love, trust, and respect to the teaching, the Sanggye, and the teachers. We focus on a white A syllable, symbolizing rigpa, awareness, in our throat energy wheel. It's very bright and radiates light and thigle. We should feel that our whole body, all our channels and nerves, are completely filled with rays and lights coming from that syllable. We should also feel that our whole body, our channels and nerves, are filled with thigles, spots of light. While we imagine this, our rigpa has to be focused on the A syllable in our throat; our rigpa should not chase after our thoughts and other spontaneously arising appearances. We also shouldn't get too deep into meditation and fall asleep. Without generating any kind of thoughts, we should try to remain in the state of emptiness, in the natural state. And we relax into sleep, continuing this awareness. According to the text, we have to be in the state of realization while we are sleeping.

Normally we have karmic dreams; dreams based on our ignorance, our emotions, and illusions. We have dreams that make us happy, unhappy, or frightened. This is because we do not realize that the dream is a just a dream. Gradually, using these practices, we can realize that our dreams are dreams, and we can change our dreams as we are dreaming them. These clear light dreams are based not on ignorance but on realization.

## Realizations of the Three Levels of Practitioner

The practitioner of high capacity will gain the ability to unify sleep and contemplation, and without any interruption, to grow the quality of the dream and attain the clear light dream. Then, the whole period of our sleep will be part of our practice of contemplation of the natural state of mind. Depending on the depth of our sleep, we will experience the appearances of the clear light dream state.

The practitioner of medium capacity will be able to realize the dream as a dream. This practitioner will remember the practice and meditate on it. Because of that realization, all illusions may even transform into the Path of Practice in the dream state. The practitioner will be able to realize that they are dreaming, that whatever is appearing in the dream is a reflection of our thought, and not chase after or attach to the dream. The practitioner can change the things that appear in the dreams that might otherwise interrupt the practice, for example, changing a tiger into a monkey.

Because we realize that we are dreaming, we can remember what our teacher has taught us and put those teachings into practice. We transform all thoughts and visions into our practice and don't attach to them or become deluded by them.

The practitioner of lower capacity may not be able to transform dualistic dream appearances into practice. But if he or she puts effort, practices enthusiastically, and prays to their root lama to be able to realize the dream as a dream, he or she may be able to realize the dream.

Normally, when we dream, it's difficult to realize it is a dream, because it appears so real and affects us. Sometimes, when we have pleasant dreams—even after opening our eyes, we wish we still had the pleasant dreams. Sometimes, we don't think they were simply dreams. Or sometimes, we have terrible dreams. We are scared, and we don't like the dream experiences. Our thoughts were fabricated by illusions, and therefore we should practice and focus our consciousness to realize those dreams as dreams, to change our view of them.

The text has described the results of three levels of capacity of the practitioner. Each of us has to judge ourselves objectively, judge our own experience and capacity, realistically, and must practice according to it, developing step by step. Then, finally, we will achieve the result of practice.

## Causes of Inability to Realize Our Dreams

If we don't realize and understand our dream as a dream, this may be because we do not understand what dreams really are. We grasp at the dreams as if they were solid. We are affected by emotions and illusions and caught up in the external projections of our mind. The text says that if we are not able to achieve any positive sign by this practice, it's because our inspiration and trust towards the Three Jewels (the teachings of Bön, the teachers, and the Sanggye) is weak. It might also mean that we don't understand the value of teachings and their essence. We may need more enthusiastic effort and more patience to continue our practice. These are faults of our mind, our inner thoughts, and we have to transform and correct them.

Other causes might be physical factors that disturb the stability of our practice. Exercise may disturb our stability and cause us to sleep too deeply or actively with too much agitation. Drinking alcohol or strong coffee, or eating certain foods before going to bed may cause us not to have any dreams at all, and if we do, the dreams wouldn't be stable, they would be disturbed. Rough physical movement and exercise, and having sexual relations, can also disturb our stability of practice.

At the beginning, it's very important to focus strongly on the visualizations and avoid all the obstacles and things that disturb us. When we first fall asleep, there are certain moments when the active manifestations that we normally clearly realize will begin to discontinue. They will normalize and become calmer. Fewer and fewer appearances will arise. We will not fall into a very deep sleep, but we will enter it with more awareness. Then, we can say that we begin to enter the practice of dream and sleep. At that time, we shouldn't try to open our eyes. Controlling our lower organs while we are falling asleep helps us in this practice.

Before we go to bed and early in the morning, it's especially helpful to pray from the core of our heart, generating trust and seeking blessings from our teacher and protector with whom we practice and are connected. We can also visualize the *yidam* and *khadro* we are practicing with dissolving into our body and seek their blessing to experience the dream of light. Gradually, our quality of sleep will develop. At first, it won't be very deep because of ignorance. But it will become much sharper, clearer, and more aware.

In the daytime, we have to focus on all the limitless visual experiences that we may face, that we perceive by the six doors of sense consciousness. We have to realize that all those appearances are part of our dream, and integrate them into our dream, so nothing remains in its own state. Whatever appearances we are experiencing, they are all a kind of dream. Whatever appears in a dream is no different from those visions. It appears, and only exists momentarily. Its quality and presence have no essence. All appearances are like dreams, and dreams are not different from appearances we experience during the day. All that we experience, sounds, feelings, taste, forms, is only momentarily there. It exists and affects us only momentarily, and then it disappears in its own way. Nothing is solid, nothing is permanent, there is nothing we can depend on, and nothing we can trust. Everything is simply there for a moment, exactly like in a dream. When a dream appears, we experience moments of pleasure and unhappiness, but the dream disappears by itself. In both cases, there is nothing we can truly rely on as being solid as we ordinarily imagine reality to be—looking at phenomena and grasping (*dagzin*) at them.

The purpose of dream practice is to free ourselves, both during the day and during the night, from grasping, holding, and attaching. We want to realize that in the essence of the phenomena, there is nothing to hold; their nature is empty. Lack of understanding of this reality, of its essence, is the source of all our problems. It's easier to realize that in a dream there is nothing to hold on to, nothing we can rely on, because we know it's just a dream. But it's very hard to realize that our daily experiences are fundamentally the same; they have no essence; they are just momentarily there; they are like a dream. There is no real difference, but our mind creates a difference between our daily experience and a dream, and we are circling in khorwa only because of a lack of understanding of the true nature, the true essence of phenomena and our own self.

That is why we always keep coming back, because we are not free from grasping, from holding. In all of us, in all common people, the grasping of subject and object is very strong. We must free ourselves from grasping to free ourselves from our ego. The teachings tell us that through practice we should show at least some change in this attitude. We practice day and night. During the day, most of our consciousness is active, and at night, most of our consciousness is not active. But in both cases, if we are not able to make any change, if our ego and our ignorance stand strong, then we are not fulfilling the essence of our practice. Therefore, it's important to try every time we can, during the daytime, to develop the awareness—even if we don't realize it deeply from inside—by thinking about the lack of truth in existence and the lack of inherent existence of this universe and of all visionary experiences.

Nothing inherently exists. When we talk to someone, it's easy to say that there is nothing to be attached to. Every one of us is good at giving this advice to others. But when it comes to following this advice ourselves, we are all beginners in kindergarten.

Some years ago in Dolanji, the father of one of the families passed away suddenly. He was quite healthy and feeling fine, so his death was a shock to everyone, especially to his wife and children. One lady from the neighborhood for several years had been practicing ngondro, and she was doing a very good practice of *chö* every day. She was comforting the widow, who was crying. Crying is very natural. When we lose someone, we cry. The woman was advising the mother not to cry, saying that it's natural, everybody has to die, we are impermanent, we will all die. She was trying to convince her that we are all impermanent and that this had to happen, so there is no reason to cry. A week later, the monks and village people were joking about her, saying that they are going to get teachings from this lady, that there is nothing to worry about, it is all impermanent.

There are two aspects to this story. The first is the lady who was advising the widow about impermanence. What made the woman realize the quality of our life and that all visual experiences are just temporal and momentary? This lady may have truly felt and realized the impermanence of life and was advising based on this experience. We cannot judge by someone's face who is a good practitioner and who is bad. It's a matter of applying our practice in life when the time comes. I think she had a true feeling of realization coming from inside of her.

The second is, we joked about it, we made fun of it, saying that one day we all have to die. We are all sure that nobody will avoid dying. There has been no one in the past, and there will be no one in the future who avoids dying; one day we will die. But we talk about it, and we don't apply it. We don't integrate it in a practical way when the time comes. We keep repeating it, but we don't practice it on our inner level. We are not trying to realize it inside; we are rather always looking outside. That's why monks, with no bad intentions, were making jokes about her.

The main point is that we must get more experience. We must get more familiar with what we are dealing with practically in our life. If we can make some changes within this environment, it will lead us more easily to deeper levels of understanding. Even if we focus on it in the dream, it will become more purposeful and meaningful.

## Progress in Dream Realization

The next parts of this session is concerned with making progress in our practice of realization in the dream. We have to realize a dream as a dream and realize that dreams are formless mental activities. Our formless mind spontaneously manifests thoughts and visions. We can transform these manifestations the way we want to. They are not solid. They are simply a mental projection of our karmic traces. Therefore, we can change them. We must understand that dream experiences are manifestations of our own mind, and they are transformable, changeable. Once we understand this, we can imagine that our whole body, all our channels and nerves, each point of our body, completely transforms into a deity with full retinue. We want to transform into the deity we know from our practice, so we may choose to transform into Yeshe Walmo, Chamma, Shenlha Ökar, or whichever deity is most familiar to us, easiest to visualize and to practice with. Gradually, we will develop a level of confidence. We will develop a meditative experience of being inseparable from the deity. We will be able to completely integrate with the deity, so that students or genuine devotees can see us as a form of the deity. It depends on how stable our concentration is and how precise our transformation into the deity is.

In the ngag tradition, there are certain methods and forms of practice of imagining ourselves as the deity of the particular practice we are performing. This means we are empowered by the deity with the power, energy, and qualities the deity has. This increases our familiarity and deepens our connection with the deity. Doing so gives us the result of liberation in the bardo state. When we realize we are in the bardo, and we are experiencing the appearance of all the visions arising, we remember the deity, our own yidam with whom we have connected and practiced for a long time. As a result of the practice and the blessing of the deity, we are able to integrate the bardo appearances into the essence of the *yidam* and liberate those appearances. This is called the liberation in the nature of the deity. We practice using this method to realize this transformation into the deity. Depending on our lifetime of practice, we may be able to use this method to transform ourselves even in the bardo.

In the ngag tradition, there are other practices that rely on transformation of visions and appearances. For example, we visualize the entire universe as a pure mandala of the deities, and we visualize each sentient being as a male or female form of *yidam* and *khadro* deities. In this way, we purify our dualistic, impure vision of others. We remove any negative thoughts about others and view them as pure and perfect. We must develop that experience until we fully view each individual as a male or female yidam or khadro. In the past, every time the great masters viewed a man or a woman, they didn't consider them as a person full of egoism, but rather as a yidam or khadro full of wisdom. They prostrated to people, seeing them as deities, whether they were realized or not. From their practice of ngag, they viewed the whole universe, all phenomena, and all beings as being pure and perfect. We can also experience and realize this view, and we can develop purity of inner perception by this practice.

Once we develop all these practices, at certain moments we will suddenly experience everything as perfectly pure, as a perfect mandala, and everyone we deal with as pure beings. Then, by practicing gradually, we will experience this even in dreams. When we develop this experience, we realize that the essence and qualities of each appearance goes back to its nature, which is emptiness; and we contemplate its nature and integrate with it. If we develop a strong realization that all phenomena are empty, then things may happen that ordinary people refer to as miracles, because they are unusual and unexpected, beyond our power. People on this level may cross through a wall without any difficulties, jump down from high cliffs, punch stones, bend iron swords, etc. All those miracles are not magical, but they come from overcoming the material conditions that limit us. For great masters, there are no conditions that limit them, because they have truly realized that the essence of everything is empty. Since it's empty, there is nothing that could bother, condition, block, or limit us. There are no obstacles, no limits to what they can or cannot do. They have no expectations or doubts of this kind. They are truly in oneness; therefore, they are capable of doing these things.

Everyone who is on this level of experience can have that kind of power. The person who has fully realized the natural state and performs these miracles has no limits. And the person who witnesses these miracles also must have a lot of inner fortune and deep realization cultivated in the past. In order to be able to see such events, we need to develop our inner spiritual practice, our faith, our trust, our realization of the nature of impermanence and of cause and result. Since many people are lacking these things nowadays, even though there are masters who have the capability to perform miracles, people don't see them much these days.

People in the West ask, why are reincarnated masters not born in the West? Why are miracles only performed in Tibet and not in the West? It's not something we can demand. We can't just say we'd like to watch a miracle. To see miracles, we must develop true trust in spiritual practice and in miracles. Only then it's possible. If a time comes when it's needed and required, then a manifestation can take place. Reincarnated masters don't reincarnate somewhere just to see the place, to check how the weather is in Italy, or to check how busy life is in America. Great masters may do something special, like perform a miracle if it is needed; but we cannot blame the masters if we do not have the wisdom to see it. When a master gives us blessing and we don't have enough wisdom to experience it, we may only feel that he touches us. We must have an inner eye; we must develop wisdom to see and feel blessings. Otherwise, we will think that the master hasn't given anything to us, and even when the master keeps giving, we will not feel that we are receiving anything.

One of the great Dzogchen masters had a conversation with his disciple. The disciple asked, "What is the essence of receiving blessings?" The teacher answered that the essence and the best way to receive blessings was to let them into our own mind. That disciple asked the master for blessings, because he had spent several years with that master, and he had to leave. The master said that he had been giving the disciple his blessings for all those years they spent together, so what new blessing should he give him now? But still he touched disciple's head with his hand. Then the master asked, "Did you receive my blessing now?" The disciple had no answer. That event opened his inner wisdom in the last moment of conversation between him and his teacher, changing his whole inner level of realization. To give and receive blessings, there are no formal conditions required. They can be received any time. But we have to be ready, and we have to receive them by our own understanding.

## Realizing When We Are Dreaming

When one realizes dreams as dreams, it's important to understand that the appearances are just visions, both in the dream and the awakened state. Through practice, we develop our inner sense and see that the dream experience is no different from the awakened experience. All existence is momentary and has no inherent essence. This is what we mean when we say the nature of everything is emptiness; not that nothing exists, but that nothing has inherent existence.

## Connecting the Practice to Daily Life

The next part of this practice is concerned with expanding our dream practice and connecting it to our daily life. To begin, we have to think of all the appearances, good and bad, beautiful and ugly, all the mountains, houses, roads, and other objects, all the visual experiences that we see. We have to understand that, in reality, they are no different than dreams. They exist only for short period, momentarily like dreams. They affect us like dreams. Sometimes, when we have good or bad dreams, they affect us, make us more joyful or frightened. It is exactly the same with all the visual experiences we encounter every day. We practice day and night to get more familiar with appearances, to get closer to their nature. In other words, the more we are familiar with the circumstances and nature of the dream, the more we are able to achieve realization in the state of the bardo after death.

When we develop some realization of the dream state, then special signs and experiences may appear. Great lamas and practitioners may connect dream signs to real life circumstances. For example, certain dreams may indicate that we will get a new job or that something will happen in our relationship or business. The lama who had such a dream may say that, because of what he saw, we may do something, or shouldn't do something, or we should do certain prayers and so on. Explaining dreams and indicating what they mean is a type of divination. Lamas have a clear level of understanding of how to connect dreams with real life circumstances. We shouldn't be too eager or to excited in connecting dreams of illusion with real life events. Most of our dreams, especially with no practice and no realization of real understanding of dreams quality, appear only because of our ignorance and karmic traces from the past. Certain circumstances and conditions cause our dreams to appear and those dreams don't indicate anything in reality.

Gradually, we develop the concept of reality being like a dream, and of our physical body being a mental body. When we sleep, our body doesn't respond, is not active, it rather remains as a continuation of our mental body. This is the way to think of our body and mind. Once we get familiar with those things, gradually we will be able to transform and change dream visions within the dream. To get to that level we must develop our dream practice. When we gain stability in our dream practice, the sign is that we can transform our dreams. When we have that familiarity, without any dualistic concepts, expectations, or doubts; when we have completely overcome all illusionary perspectives; when we realize the truth of reality, that ultimately everything is inseparable from emptiness; and when we are unified with, and rest in, the mother nature of all; then we are completely in the natural state.

We talk about four activities: eating, sleeping, sitting and walking. We eat in that state, we sleep in that state, we sit in that state, and we walk in that state. Even though we are carrying on these daily experiences, at a deep level we continue in the realization of the true nature of mind. We are not separate from the state of realization. We have brought that state into these daily activities, and continue in that state, so that every moment and every daily activity becomes practice.

Terton Guru Nontse, one of the great, well-known Dzogchen masters, one day had manifested himself as a wild animal. He met three hunters, who tried to hunt some animals. They couldn't catch anything, so they were hungry and tired. Guru Nontse, to help them and to fulfill their desire, manifested in the form of a tiger. In his tiger form, he killed animals and brought them to the hunters to eat. When he came to the hunters, he looked like a human being.

At some level of realization, we are able to transform not only in the dream state, but also in waking life. And when we get great familiarity with the dream state and are able to transform there, then our physical body is resisting on the level of elements and materials it is composed of. But on the inner level, once we realize all phenomena are just manifestations from the base of emptiness, kunzhi, the mother, that the nature of the phenomena are inseparable from the nature of the base, and that phenomena are unified in the base, then we are in the natural state. There are no longer any conditions or barriers. And such manifestations can take place. Guru Nontse performed them. When he got together with the hunters and started preparing the meat to eat, one of the hunters saw that Guru Nontse has some animal hair left between his teeth. He didn't say a word about this, but he thought to himself that the lama might have killed the animal himself. The lama immediately realized that the hunter had the wrong view. So the lama collected all the bones, wrapped them in the animal's skin, and snapped his fingers. Then, the animal they were eating stood before them and ran away.

When our mind is truly beyond any barriers, then such things can happen. We are manifesting everything by our mind. It's not just thinking and wishing something to happen, but real transformation. These are not just stories, but real facts. This master was born from a mother, but he has never died; instead, he dissolved himself into his own statue. In his appearance, he was a great hunter. He had two hunting dogs and every day he went to the forest to hunt, and every evening he crushed ants with a stone. In the ordinary view, he was a hunter. But we only see that he killed those animals. We can't see that in fact he was liberating them, transforming them from the animal realm into higher spiritual realms. At the end of his life he made his own statue from clay. He would ask people who were passing through, who the statue was similar to. Different people gave different answers. At last a person came who said that it looked exactly like him, like Guru Nontse. Then, in front of that person, he dissolved into that sculpture with his two dogs. Until the Chinese came, the statue of him with two hunting dogs remained in Tibet. There were prophecies made by great lamas, who said that whoever met this lama, or at least got a blessing by touching his sculpture, will never be reborn in lower realms.

The Sanggye manifest in the form they want to, not because of ignorance, but because of compassion. They manifest only for the purpose of helping sentient beings. We can also transform in this way when our mind is truly realized and achieves its true essence, because there is no difference in our natures. The difference is only in appearances, according to our deluded view. What we see in front of us depends completely on the capacity of our eyes. We see only raw material, we see a person as just a person, a mountain as just mountain, a tree as just a tree, but we don't see their true nature. And we are not doing anything to integrate the nature of two existing objects. For great masters who have realized such a level of experience, the vision or material view doesn't make much difference. Therefore, they can transform stone into gold or water into *dütsi* (healing essence); they simply transform it. This is because nothing has solid existence, nothing exists as one form, nothing exists as we perceive it. It's all a matter of our view, of our mind and our inside.

Even in ordinary life, we can give two or three definitions or names to one person. The same person may be seen as good by someone, as bad by someone else, and still other people will think of him or her as neither good nor bad. We give those titles according to what our mind thinks, according to our very limited judgment.

In reality, this person is neither good nor bad. An object is only good for a person who thinks it is good, but it is not inherently good. It is the same with being bad. This is how our mind thinks, how our dualistic concepts and thoughts delude us and make us carry on this illusion of existence.

With this understanding, we should practice our awareness in the dream state in order to realize the nature of visions and appearances. If we recognize that what we are having is just a momentarily appearing dream, we can change the dream the way we want to. If we can do this in the dream, then we can transform our dreams and sleep, and change them into the pathway to enlightenment. We should gradually practice this way, judging ourselves to what extent we can do so.

If we are not able to realize dreams as dreams, nor transform or change dream forms, then there are some methods that can help us. They are not an absolute solution, but a way to force the experience. In our body, there are special channels and nerves on the left side of our neck, which people check to see if someone is alive or not. If we press those nerves, people may fall unconscious; if we press it for too long, the person would die. So we may press these nerves to help others fall asleep, but we should make sure that we know exactly how to do it, and that there is someone else with us who could help us if needed. Otherwise, it may be dangerous. But this serves only to force the experience when we are not able to achieve any level of dream experience by all those gradual steps and methods. While we practice this forceful method, with the awareness of inner visual experiences, we may be able to reach the realization of the dream state. But the text clearly states that if it's too long or too strong, then we will pass away. That's why it's important to know exactly how to do this and to have someone with us. The best way is to experience this realization without using this method; it's safer.

We should practice the dream method described in this eleventh session until we experience one of the three results of experience. The students of high capacity, when they have a dream, will be able to liberate it within its own state, without force or effort. When the dream arises, at the same time, it liberates in the natural state of mind.

The practitioners of medium capacity will realize the dream as a dream. If we are not able to liberate the dream in its own state when it appears, what we call "self-liberation," then we can liberate it by understanding that the dream is a dream. This means simply that we will realize that everything that we experience is like a dream, and we will not be deluded. We will not grasp; we will not attach to pleasant dreams and be frightened by tragedies in bad dreams. We will understand them all as dreams, that they exist only momentarily, and that there is nothing to grasp, to hold, or to be attached to. This way, we prevent the continuation of the growth of ignorance in the dreams.

The practitioners of lower capacity, who are not able to achieve these experiences, can understand dreams as dreams through reasoning. We simply think and reason that the dream has no quality of independent existence and only affects us because of our dualistic thoughts. We must analyze the fact that dreams exists only momentarily and do not have inherent existence. Analytical reasoning helps us to see that dreams are unstable, have no strength, and no way to affect our life. They have only a momentary life—a momentary existence—and have no power to affect us as we perceive it.

We live in a great theatre, watching the manifestations of our own mind, caused by ignorance. Even when we look at the same thing, we have different concepts of what we see. It's like our whole life is a drama performed in a theatre. When our life ends, the drama ends, and people say that someone has passed away. People pray for him, for a few days talk about him and explain how nice, bad, or good he was. Month by month and year by year, the memories fade, and people are concerned with other things. This repeats all the time, and we are not going to change. At the end, we will go through the same thing. We will have to say that it's now time for us to say goodbye and go.

This is how our life goes. We carry on our daily activities, day in and day out, and we are caught up in the drama without knowing exactly which of the things we do will bring us benefit for the bardo and the next life. We complain about it, but still we keep doing the same things. This is how our worldly life exists. We should go back and reflect on what in our worldly life makes any sense to us.

Let's now focus on the visual experiences we have, trying to see their qualities as I have mentioned before, unstable as a dream, as an illusion, a magical performance, truthless. After searching it we cannot find any essence in it, but still we are deluded by it, we are chasing it. What is the source of these qualities and experiences? We should meditate on this question.

We should practice every day. Daily practice helps us overcome our ignorance and illusions, so we can break the pattern of circulating in this drama of our life. Without some stable realization of the true essence, true quality, true nature of life and mind, we go in circles, moment after moment, day after day, year after year. We never reach our point, the realization of the natural state of mind and all the phenomena of the existing universe. We talk about the natural state of mind because it's directly connected with us, but if we looked at any things that surround us—mountains, elements, our friends, buildings—it all has its source in the nature of mind. It's important to realize this; otherwise we will keep circulating in the same state, in the same surroundings.

We have six aspects of consciousness and five aggregates to experience, to feel. We perceive forms with our eyes, we hear sounds with our ears, we smell with our nose, taste with our tongue, we feel what's rough and what's soft with our body. Every time those five aggregates are activated, for example, when we see something that seems beautiful to us, and we think it's very nice, we generate attachment. We don't think about the sources of the perceived phenomenon. We don't think that it is truthless, not inherently existing, changeable, unreliable. Rather, we see only the beauty of this object.

That beautiful appearance gets into contact with our eyes and goes to our mind consciousness. Our mind consciousness makes a decision and says that something is good or bad. If our mind says it is good, we attach to it. If our mind says it is bad, we push away from it. That decision leaves a trace. That's how we leave karmic traces, which are stored in the kunzhi. And this is how we keep circulating repeatedly. Those prints don't disappear. The prints, good and bad, positive and negative, are stored in the kunzhi. The prints remain in the kunzhi until the right conditions and circumstances arise, and then those traces manifest themselves. This is why we say that all the negative experiences coming from ignorance and illusion will manifest one day, in their own time, and will affect ourselves, not anyone else.

In the same way as attachment, we generate anger. When we encounter an object that looks good to us and seems nice, we generate love and attachment. When we met someone who we don't appreciate, who is not so interesting, not exciting, perhaps ugly, then we say that he or she is ugly, this or that is not good, not perfect, and we act accordingly. When we look, for example, at a girl who we think is beautiful, we are just commenting on how she looks on the outside. We talk about her face and body that we see. We build our definitions on whatever we see with our material eyes only. But we don't see her inner beauty or ugliness, we don't see her anger, desire, hatred.

When we say "good" or "bad," and we attach or push away accordingly, then we are led astray by our temporary views. We are not thinking about anything more than is presented to us. What I say here is that, of course, we should enjoy things. We shouldn't give up everything and become monks. We should enjoy life, but within limits; and we should understand the nature of phenomena and take some momentary advantage of them, but remaining aware of where we are, without getting lost in them, without losing our control.

The teachings in this part teach us to experience external visions or to go into the dream and compare them, to see how they are different and what we can learn from this. Why is it so important to understand a dream as a dream? Why is it important to understand that external visions are only momentarily there and have no inherent existence? We practice this to free ourselves, to liberate ourselves. But, we are at the point where we are always complaining, we are deluded, ruled by the five poisons. It all comes from our ignorance, and this ignorance manifests because we are nurturing these visions with our emotions and holding them with our thoughts as if they were real. We grasp them and hold them without understanding their nature. When we realize that they are simply a projection of our own mind, without independent existence, then our self-grasping thoughts and egoism will naturally weaken and detach. This will relieve our grasping and release our egoism, and we will open to wisdom. That's what we are seeking.

SESSION 12

# Integration of External Phenomena

This is the twelfth session. This session is concerned with our external visions and appearances in the daytime. The text begins this session by quoting several different Dzogchen texts.

## Detaching from Sensory Perceptions

One of the texts that is quoted says we should practice without chasing after the five sense objects. The five sense objects are form (sight), sound (hearing), smell, taste, and feeling (touch). There are five aspects of consciousness that perceive those five objects. The text says we should practice without chasing the five objects.

What does this mean? Naturally, when we perceive something with our senses, we have contact with it. Our sense consciousness recognizes the object we perceive. The text doesn't mean we should not look or feel or respond to what we perceive. It means that we should not grasp or attach to these perceptions. We shouldn't chase after them. Attachment and chasing come from thinking the perceptions are solid forms with inherent existence. In reality, they don't have inherent existence. They exist only momentarily. We perceive them, we give them definitions, and we judge them as good or bad, beautiful or ugly. Every attachment, every act of grasping at objects beyond their reality, is called ignorance. Ignorance hides the true nature of the object we perceive.

Instead, when we perceive something with our senses, we should not think of the perceptions as separate, inherently existing objects. In our normal way, we have a strong sense of the concept of the inherent existence of subject and object. We should free ourselves of the concept of subject and object.

How do we detach from objects? The text says that it is difficult to detach from objects, because we are familiar with attaching to material conditions. It's our habit. When we begin to attach to something, we should first try not to follow the attachment. Immediately, we try to reverse it by realizing the true nature of the object. If we see a beautiful garden, our body feels the joy coming from being in this surrounding. The smell and sight of trees, flowers, and herbs gives us pleasure. We feel this way because we are only viewing the garden generally, without going further into details of how those plants are growing, how long it will exist, and when the plants will die. We are not looking into the nature of its existence; we are simply attaching to its beauty. The feeling of happiness and peace that appears in our mind comes from contact with different sense objects through our eyes. This gives us a message, and our mind accepts it for a moment. But while we benefit from such circumstances, while we are inspired by them, while we appreciate them and accept the comfort coming from them, we also have to remember that these are all impermanent. They have no true inherent existence. It's all momentarily there, and none of it is permanent.

Within the state of that realization, we may enjoy and benefit from the garden and the feelings it gives us. Every material object, every existing condition, including ourselves, remains in that state of nature; nothing is permanent, trustworthy, reliable, nothing has solid form. But still, we don't ignore its benefits. We accept them, according to our dualistic judgment, although they are only momentary. This is what the text means when it advises us not to attach to or detach from material existence.

Everything is within its own limit of untruthfulness. We lead our day-to-day lives in the state of our "normal" perception of reality. The text tells us that every action of our sense organs and consciousness should not be left in our normal way of perceiving material conditions. Every moment, we have to be fully aware of the reality of every phenomenon. If we keep in that state, then we are connecting everything into practice. Our ordinary, dualistic thought is transformed into the path of awareness, and we are on the path to enlightenment.

But if somehow we do get attached, then we have to reverse the attachment by considering its true nature. And we want to try not to leave karmic prints behind, which would strengthen those attachments. We should keep these three steps in mind: (i) do not get attached; (ii) if we are attached, be aware of it, and try to reverse the concept of attachment by realizing that it has no essence—that, in reality, nothing can be held by attachment; and (iii) if we are attached, we shouldn't have a strong attachment, as a strong attachment may leave strong karmic traces or imprints.

## Continuous Practice

We need to develop our practice gradually and continuously. We've all had the experience that our practice goes smoothly for a month or so, meditating, reciting prayers, doing practices. But then, we enter a phase of practice where, during meditation, lots of ideas arise. We think that we have to call someone, check something, get up and do something to interrupt our practice. This occurs because we are getting more sensitive, our practice is improving, and our inner wisdom is developing. Now, we have to decide who will win: our inner wildness or our wisdom. We need to be mindful and patient. When we are not able to control our wildness, then we should recite the prayer of lamé naljor and pray to the teachers and protectors, seeking blessings to control the wildness and calm ourselves down. This phase will also not remain forever, it will change after some time, and then we will strongly stabilize. This is how we progress gradually.

# Three Levels and Three Methods

The teachings always talk about three levels of advancement: the highest, medium, and lowest.

On the highest level, the text speaks of self-arising and self-liberation, and gives the example of snow falling on the ocean. When the snow falls on the ocean, it melts and becomes water itself. This happens because the nature of the snow is water, so it is unified in its essence. In the same way, when we realize the natural state, the nature of cause, of existence, of links and connections, we can immediately liberate everything by itself. Snow melts into water and becomes one with the ocean, because of the causes and conditions of snow and water. In the same way, when we experience anger, we can liberate it, because we understand its cause, conditions, and result. Instead of allowing anger to manifest into action, if we let it be, it will liberate itself. This liberation happens without any effort, without any chasing, without looking for a method of antidote, or anything else. Just let it be, and anger disappears by itself. In the same way, everything liberates itself. This is how we can integrate and liberate all appearances on the higher level of realization.

On the second level, when we are not able to let phenomena liberate by themselves, we can apply a method of overcoming attachment and the five poisons. When a feeling arises, we simply focus on the feeling, on where it appears on who is experiencing the feeling, on who is reacting to the feeling. We analyze the feeling as mentioned above and try to look for the face of the feeling. The feeling will liberate itself. Through this method, we can eliminate the power of the poison.

For example, when we close our eyes and begin meditation, all kinds of appearances start to arise. We try to force them not to appear, but they still keep coming. Sometimes we chase them, and they don't remain there. They keep changing moment after moment. Like on television news programs, where there is someone telling the main story, but at the bottom of the screen, a printed strip of other news is always moving. Our thoughts continuously come, one after another. Although we may want one thought to remain, it changes; although we may want to not have them, they still come. If we suddenly look back straight at them and consider who watches them, who experiences them, when we try to see his face directly, then we will be able to dissolve all these appearances and distracting thoughts. By looking directly or closely at these appearances and thoughts, by just being still in that experience without any judgment, all these appearances will dissolve into the nature of themselves.

On the third level, we apply the method of the antidote, to temporarily detach ourselves from grasping and attachment. To apply the antidote, we go back to our inner world, where both the appearances, and the thoughts that observe them, arise spontaneously. There is a subject and object that we experience inside: the objects appear all the time, and the subject always watches them. If we look at these two forms, we will see that they appear spontaneously, without stopping, and are very unstable. We have to ask ourselves a question and see how fast they are moving and changing from moment to moment.

It's the same with external visions. At first glance, it seems that everything exists the way we see it—solid, formed, present. There seems to be no reason to see external objects as impermanent. When we see a beautiful garden, it is there, we can see it, and it seems that it is solid. When we see a snow mountain and take a rough look at it, and it's hard to think that it's there only momentarily. It's the same way with all material things. When we go to the supermarket, we see all the groceries and everyday items gathered there. We don't think that these items are momentary. This happens because we are seeing on a very shallow level. We look at the name that we give to those objects, and it overshadows and covers their nature. We're not going into their reality. If we go into the real source of every phenomenon, be it a garden, a mountain, a person, all materials, if we search each and every thing, if we seek to identify its real form as it is named, we will not find anything. If we chase them, we will find nothing. If we go to their source, we will find nothing. We will always find only space, emptiness, which is their real source, real nature. No matter how big the snow mountain is, how beautiful the girl is, how handsome the man is, their true nature is just emptiness. The appearance of form is only momentary; there is nothing solid there at all. If you think carefully, you will find out that there is nothing solid at all, as we perceive it. But still, we so strongly try to grasp it.

The main point here is to try to understand these three levels of our inner growth. At the beginning, we can at least try to apply the third stage. We start with applying reason and analysis, thinking about examples and applying their meaning. The teachings always give examples so that we can understand their meaning more easily. When we understand the example, then we can apply its meaning. The teachings in the text give reasons and methods of decreasing our ignorance and the attachment to inner and outer objects, and give us examples to help us—by thinking they are as a dream, a magical performance, and by thinking about their changeable, unstable, transforming quality. All these things, if we are aware of them all the time, affect us. We call it a strength of continuation. When we realize something, but we keep forgetting about it, there is no continuation, and we will not develop the strength of continuous progress. We progress through understanding and continuing our practice by active meditation and remembering what we have understood. That leads to inner development and realization.

We have to practice this way until we get an experience of all existence and all visionary appearances as an empty form. All appearances manifest within this emptiness, and this emptiness and the appearances are inseparable; they are two aspects of one form. The teachings introduce the visionary appearances as the self-manifestation part of our mind. Within the self-manifestation of our mind, in the state of emptiness, visions appear. And these continuously appearing visions are empty. This inseparability is called unification of emptiness and appearances. If we develop this realization, then we can close our eyes, and without much effort, immediately say, "Yes, this is in fact real." We have to develop this kind of feeling. This way, we are not only detaching from external phenomena, but on every level of understanding and development, it will completely change the level of the five poisons that are bothering us, and the wisdom we expect will automatically develop. No special place for wisdom is required, and no special place for poison is required. Both are in one state; within their nature, they are unified. Everything appears within the state of emptiness. The appearances themselves are empty. As we practice, the experience of perceiving two forms, the empty nature and the form of appearances, diminishes. We see that the concepts of subject and object—of visionary appearances and empty nature—these two aspects have no separate existence. They are integrated into oneness.

# The Integration of Inner Appearances

The thirteenth session is mainly about bringing our experiences, our dualistic thoughts and visions, into practice.

The text tells us how to transform our ordinary thoughts into practice. According to one of dho texts quoted here, "the moment we see ignorance is the moment rigpa arises." This sentence contains the full essence of the teachings.

Another Dzogchen text says that after you renounce the five poisons, there is no separate form of wisdom; everything is within the natural state without renouncing anything. There is no wisdom after renouncing ignorance and the five poisons; without renouncing anything, everything is perfected within this state.

When we realize ignorance and its nature, in this realization, rigpa is present. They are not two separate objects. The moment we realize the nature of ignorance is the moment we awaken. We are deluded, and we are circling in this world of suffering because we didn't see and realize ignorance. We understand ignorance, we are aware of it, but we do not realize it. Only because of that, we are circling in khorwa, continuously turning the wheel of suffering.

As we have seen earlier, the goal of the teachings is to discover the true state of mind. Discovering the true state of mind means overcoming ignorance. Overcoming ignorance means awakening the state of rigpa. Awakening the state of rigpa means integrating our awareness into the true natural state of mind, like the mother and child seeing each other after a long absence. When the mother (the Nature of Mind) and the child (rigpa) are unified into oneness, we call that realization.

Everything we perceive "normally," so-called ignorance or so-called wisdom, everything we name, is just a way that our mind functions. In the West, people talk about the "brain," but in Bön, we talk about the "mind." All of these things we perceive and name depend on the mind. That's what the text means when it says, "there is no wisdom when we renounce the five poisons." In the Dzogchen view, there is nothing to renounce, and there is nothing to ignore; we simply have to realize and discover. We don't have to expend all this effort. We simply need to realize and discover the natural state. Everything is in the natural state.

Dho, ngag, and Dzogchen all talk about removing ignorance and freeing ourselves from the five poisons. There are different methods to achieve this, depending on the capacity of the student. The dialectic, philosophical way of dho is based on applying the antidotes; wisdom is the antidote to ignorance, love and kindness to anger, flexibility and openness to hatred, generosity to attachment and desire, etc. Every time something negative arises, we need the opposite of it. The dho method is good for some people. But according to Dzogchen, when we apply the dho method, we are not freeing ourselves but trapping ourselves in the dualistic trap by adding more thoughts. The ngag tradition has a method of transforming each poison into wisdom, transforming our physical body into the deity, transforming our energy into the power and positive energy of the deity.

In Dzogchen, we eliminate those negative, dualistic thoughts without any effort on our side, by letting them self-liberate, eliminate by themselves. The text gives an example of a man who is searching for jewels. He crosses the ocean and has to face many challenges and difficult circumstances. For us practitioners, the most valuable jewel is the discovery of our Nature of Mind. The way across the ocean to find the jewels is a metaphor for crossing the ocean of khorwa to discover our Nature of Mind. We have to face and pass through the dualistic thoughts and obstacles. To find the jewel, we need to have the patience and persistence to cross the whole way and reach our destination. In each moment, we have to be aware and patient. Just as treasure hunters who search for jewels have protection from the enemies who could attack them, we also need the protection of patience to deal with all the dualistic thoughts and views, and other experiences that arise because of our five poisons and illusory views.

In Dzogchen, we have to be completely free from the concept of applying a method of antidote to eliminate the ignorance. We do not depend on any of the methods of antidotes; rather, we eliminate obstacles only by our own realization and leaving everything to self-liberate. We should also free ourselves from the concept that there is something to eliminate and something else to receive. Dzogchen says we have to be free from both the concept of renouncing obstacles and the concept of applying antidotes. Only then are we able to overcome obstacles by themselves. The text gives the example of the ocean and its waves. Waves arise within the ocean, and their quality is water. They are not separate from the ocean itself. They arise, decrease and dissolve within the ocean itself, inseparable from it. In the same way the stars arise in the sky, the sun and moon arise during day and night. All arise within the space of the sky and dissolve within that space. Within the space of the Nature of Mind, all the appearances of thoughts and imaginations, positive and negative, all the appearances in the inner and outer world appear within their space and dissolve within space.

We've discussed that the word *Dzogchen* consists of two words: *dzog*, meaning everything is "perfect," everything is "complete;" and the word *chen*, meaning "great, huge, limitless." Dzogchen, the "great perfection," teaches that everything is perfect and complete within the natural state. It's not perfect because we created it intentionally with our thoughts; it's perfected within itself. It arises in its own way, because it is spontaneously perfect, so it's spontaneously arising. Dzogchen teachings advise us to stop searching and just realize.

The text tells a story relating to how we, sentient beings, do not discover and realize our own Nature of Mind, even though we have never been separated from it. The story is of an old woman who considered herself to be the poorest person in the village. She had no house, no place to live, no belongings. She lived in a cave, and every day she begged for food on the streets. One day a stranger passing through noticed that she was living in a cave full of gold ore. He asked her why she was living in such a poor way. She answered that she owned nothing and was dependent on people's generosity. He said that she was the richest person in the area. She got angry and thought that he was making fun of her poverty, but he insisted that she was rich. She asked him how it was possible, if she owned nothing. He told her that the cave she lived in was made of gold ore, and none of the people living in houses had such a treasure. Then he told her that the rock of her cave could be turned to gold using certain methods. The old lady had lived day and night in a golden cave, but she didn't realize it was golden. She was begging and suffering, thinking that she was the poorest person in the area. She didn't realize she had a golden house, much more valuable than houses of all the village people.

It's the same with us. We are always within the natural state of mind, and it has never been far from us, but we haven't realized its perfection and qualities. Everything exists within it, but still we search for Nature of Mind somewhere else. The person who showed the old woman that the rock is gold is a teacher who has experience of realization of his or her own natural state of mind. The rock cave where the old woman lived without ever realizing that it was made of gold is ourselves. We live in the perfect natural state of mind, but we have never realized it and never discovered the perfect, pure quality of Nature of Mind.

The point is that we shouldn't try to search outside, but we should look inside. Bön always says that our inner mirror is the best way to see our inside. The outer mirror that we have in our bathroom won't give us a reflection of our inside. Every day, in the morning and in the evening, we shouldn't forget to pray to Tonpa Shenrab and the protectors, and mainly to our teachers. We should ask for blessings to discover, to understand and realize our true state of mind; seek the blessings to open our inner awareness, to remove the darkness of ignorance, to discover and see the inner beauty of the natural state of mind.

We should seek it by true, genuine prayer coming from inside, not just repeating words like a tape recorder. The tape recorder doesn't understand the words it repeats. It doesn't reflect on them but simply repeats them. We must not be like that. When we recite prayers, we should make sure they are coming from our inside, to connect and seek the blessing in a pure and true way. If we are able to truly connect, the manifestation of blessings, protection, and power, whatever we seek, will always come to us directly, without any obstacles. As long as our state of inner awakening is completely pure and has no stain of influence of any negativities and poisons, there is a possibility that the awakened state will arise, and we will achieve realization.

When we are meditating and focusing, we see that appearances seem to become more active. We have them all when we are not practicing, but we see them more clearly during meditation, because when we are in meditation, it is like being in clear water that we can look through and see whatever is in it, like fishes and stones. Normally, we don't see those inner appearances as clearly as in meditation, because we are like dirty, stirred water. When we stir the water, mud arises, and we don't see anything. Our ignorance and dualistic energies are shaken inside us, and we can only see the negative aspects and energies of poisons, rather than the wisdom aspect.

The method of Dzogchen is like a farmer's scythe that cuts many weeds with one movement. We don't need to cut all the weeds one by one. Without any extra effort, by applying one big blade, we cut all the weeds along the way. Once we cut the main source, we cut everything. That main source is ignorance. If we completely take out ignorance, which is the root of the five poisons, then its manifestations have no chance to arise.

In Dzogchen teachings, we always focus on the Nature of Mind, because when we discover our own mind and its nature, then we don't have to examine every phenomena and check what its nature is, whether it's empty or not. We realize the nature of all phenomena by realizing our true Nature of Mind. That's why it's more important to realize our own Nature of Mind than to attempt to realize the nature of all other phenomena.

# Introduction of Appearances as Mind

When we look at our conditions, material surroundings, all the phenomenal existence, we see that there is nothing that is not connected to the mind. Everything is a manifestation of our mind. A quotation from another Dzogchen text says that all the visual experiences we see in front of our eyes, everything that we see surrounding us, appears in the mind and from the mind. And this mind itself is rootless, endless, and boundless. So the appearances are also rootless and truthless, nothing exists in them inherently. Therefore, we can experience the appearances of deities and enlightened realms. We should experience everything with authoritative understanding that all the existing phenomena appear as the manifestation of our true mind. Every aspect, good or bad, happiness or sorrow, positive or negative, beautiful or ugly depends on our decision. We perceive and experience things according to our mind.

When we think about *khorwa* and *nyangde*, suffering and enlightenment, we feel they are two separate objects, solid and independent. But when we look into ourselves more precisely, in a detailed way, to search for their root, instead of finding a solid form of khorwa or nyangde, we simply find the connection to our mind, to our karmic traces reflected in the mind itself. It doesn't mean that the Nature of Mind is creating both suffering and happiness. It's not. It's not creating them, but rather they are a reflection of the mind's own thoughts, according to the causes and conditions.

Both khorwa and nyangde appear as manifestations of the natural state. From our normal, unrealized perspective, we see two different forms: khorwa and nyangde. Because our natural state of mind has this potential of manifestation, it's possible to manifest them, but the name, the title of "khorwa" and "nyangde," depends on how we see and conceptualize these two objects. When we realize the true Nature of Mind, we say that we have achieved realization, enlightenment; when we are deluded and do not realize the natural state, we call ourselves deluded, because we are under the influence of ignorance, and we generate the manifestations of khorwa. Therefore, these two objects appear as manifestations, but they are not a part of the natural state itself. In the natural state, there is no duality, no khorwa and nyangde, there is only oneness, single point, where everything is perfect.

When we practice, first we understand it, then experience it, then realize it, then gradually, signs will come that we can integrate with the nature, without the boundaries of our ordinary, common view. When we experience and realize it, it will make us much more open. We will see everything as a reflection of our own nature. Once we have the full power and authority to see in this way, then our mind will be able to transform everything, transform the way things are by transforming how our mind sees them. Simply by focusing on it, we can transform stone or sand into gold, fire into energy, water into *dütsi*, because inherently, nothing exists. When we don't realize it, we experience the hell realms and sufferings of other realms. When we realize it, then we will no longer suffer in the six realms; we achieve enlightenment. It's only a matter of whether we have realized it or not. The Dzogchen view says that the difference between khorwa and nyangde is between realizing and not realizing this nature. It's not enough only to talk about this realization; we need to experience it truly from the inside. When we are not in a state of realization, for example in the bardo, then our karmic traces arise and we follow them. When we realize our nature, we are able to integrate these karmic traces, and once we integrate them, we will not follow them, but they will discontinue and dissolve into their own nature.

Once, a great Dzogchen master was practicing and had a dream. In this dream, he thought he was in hell, experiencing the suffering of the hell realm. At the beginning, he was very afraid and agitated by the experience of that suffering. Then, in the dream, he realized that he was in the bardo, experiencing the sufferings of the hell realm. Because of this realization, he remembered his teacher and the teachings he received, which said that if we could achieve inner realization, then even the suffering of the hell realms would be experienced as joy. The moment he reflected on this essence taught by his teacher and shifted his view accordingly, that same moment he was free from the suffering of the hell realm. That's how the way we view or grasp things may change them. We grasp and hold things, but when we ask who is viewing or holding, and who is deluded, everything comes back to our mind. Therefore, the teachings say that everything is connected with the mind.

Some scholars from the Gelugpa tradition misunderstand when we say that everything is connected with the mind. They say that means that Dzogchen believes in creation—believes that the universe was created. It's not so. Dzogchen doesn't accept the creation of the universe, of khorwa, by our mind, but views them as a manifestation. There is a difference between creation and manifestation. Appearances of these experiences in dreams, in the bardo, or in the wakeful state, all are connected directly with our own Nature of Mind. They are all just reflections of our own nature.

Different beings perceive the same object differently. For example, when humans look at water, they see water. Beings from the hell realm see it differently, and hungry ghosts see it differently. We look at the world and experience it in different ways, according to the views held by our minds. We make definitions of beauty and ugliness, of what's good and bad, but they are judgments made by our mind, according to our own view. There is no objective basis for this judgment. If "beauty" existed objectively, then all people would judge it the same way, everyone would see it as equally beautiful. But the same thing appears different to different people. We use these examples because we can relate to them, and they help us understand. There is no single person who is always good, and no single person who is always bad. Someone may be always good or always bad according to our view and judgment, but our reasoning doesn't apply to everyone. Your reasons may not be applicable to me, and my reasons may not be applicable to you. That shows that there is no inherent truth of the particular object— just the definition we give it.

When we say "I," we mean our mind, our inner concepts. When we say, "I'm happy," or "I'm not happy," it is also our own limited judgment, our reasons based on our feelings. When our inner feelings tell us we are satisfied and happy, then we agree with them and think we are happy. When we tell someone that we are unhappy and upset, they might not care about it. But for us, it means a lot. If we have an inner burden, we are not happy. This is a judgment based on our inside; it manifests from inside. Outer events are only temporary conditions, temporary support.

When the text talks about introducing visions, appearances, what we see and feel as our mind, it means just what we are doing right now, explaining how they are connected to us. We are not free from sorrow and unhappiness, because we have not understood this real connection. Therefore, we are in trouble, not happy or satisfied.

When we try to realize the true Nature of Mind, we cannot ignore external conditions and attempt to find something solely from inside. We are connected with external appearances and our nature. All these appearances are nothing else but reflections of our nature, of the base of all, *kunzhi chang chub kyi sem*, of our mind. The mind we talk about here is not the solid mind of dho and ngag. Here we are talking according to the Dzogchen view of the *kunzhi chang chub kyi sem*, the enlightened mind, which is the base of all. Again, this is not the enlightened mind we talk about in preliminary practices or in dho; we talk about the kunzhi, which is the base of all knowledge. *Kunzhi* means "the base of all;" *kun* means "all;" *zhi* means "base." *Chang chub* means "enlightened," "purified," or "perfected." *Sem* means "mind (enlightened mind)." When, in Dzogchen teachings, we talk about the awareness of mother and son, kunzhi is this mother. We are not talking about the mind that is busy and active; all these activities are manifesting within kunzhi.

This kunzhi is the base of all, because everything manifests within it. Until we discover and realize this kunzhi as the base of all manifestations and appearances, then all our visions are like illusions. When we drive a car in summer, in the far distance we may see water on the road. Until we realize this is just a mirage appearing because of the heat, we might think that there really is water. That is an example of illusion. There is a sickness that causes a person to see a snow mountain as yellow. Snow is not yellow, but the sickness affects our sight, so we see snow as yellowish. We may also mistakenly view the rope lying on the road as a snake. This is how we get deluded; this is our illusionary inner connection to the material things we deal with.

When we go deeper inside, we see that this deluded perception is based on our illusions and our distinguishing of "self," "me," "my," "others," "good," "bad," "enemies," and "friends." We do it because we have not realized that our concepts and reactions to external things are in fact responses to our own manifestations. We rather think that there are two solid, independent objects standing in front of each other, opposing each other, and reacting to each other. If we are always far away from the true essence of reality, then every moment of our life will be based on grasping, ignorance, and illusion. We will experience ourselves as happy or sorrowful, but this is all based on our own illusion.

It's important to know the natural state of mind, but to make this understanding deeper, more reliable, and stable, it's important to understand how much we are tied up with our everyday appearances of cyclic existence, how we can overcome this connection, and how we can discontinue the functioning of khorwa.

Think about what I just stated—how is everything connected— and reflect on ourselves. What do we think of ourselves? If I'm looking at you and you are looking at me, the looking is same, but we have different views. You think I'm here independently; I have independent, objective existence, because you see my body here. I look at you, and think you exist objectively. This is our common concept of how we are connected. But if we looked deeper, to the reality of this connection, to see what exactly it is, then it would look different from our common perspective.

What is the connection between the base and the manifestation? What are the differences between them? The text says that everything that we see from our viewpoint is not the how things really exist, only how we view them. The lack of understanding of that reality is the cause of our circling and suffering in this khorwa. We don't like it, but we are still here, suffering. Therefore, it's important to realize that this is all like a dream. Dzogchen doesn't ignore or deny the existence of phenomena. Dzogchen says that it's important to understand phenomena as they are, not as we wish they were. When we realize that, we get proof that it is in fact truthless and sourceless—that it lacks independent, inherent existence. One of the important Dzogchen texts says, "Rootless nature of existence—way you view, you see as it is." That means, the way we look makes a difference. As I mentioned earlier, we say that someone is so good, because we make him so by our judgment, not because he really is so himself. "Rootless nature" means that nothing exists truly and independently. Why is it rootless, sourceless, without independent, inherent existence? If we search whatever object we believe is solidly there: ourselves, our mind, or anything else; if we search for the root of it, the reality of it, what will we find? We can analyze any example, any object that we think is solid and exists from its own side. But in reality, we do not find any confirmed ground or root; thus it is called "rootless." So, where does it come from?

Our so-called mind is a very strong feeling we all have: "I," "me," "myself." We can die for it, kill for it, destroy for it. We do everything for this so called "me." If we care and worry so much for this "I," we treat it so sincerely and defend it so strongly, first we have to find out how valuable this "I" is, and where it exists. If we don't even know how valuable our "I" is, how can we do things for it? It's like shooting an arrow in the darkness without seeing what we are aiming at. If we shoot an arrow in the darkness, we are not certain if it will hit the right spot. Until we realize our Nature of Mind, the connection we were talking about is like that. We lose our focus, the point we try to focus on.

And the same is true with our daily life. We think it's very serious; we think our relationships are serious; we think our connection with a friend is serious; we think our material concerns are serious. We think everything exists as we see it and that it was there, is there, and will remain there. We don't think it's temporarily there. We live in an illusion, but we don't realize it. We are distracted but we don't notice it, we don't see clearly how and when it happens. We can understand it only when we are more mindful, more aware and awake.

I mentioned earlier about how nothing is inherently good or bad, beautiful or ugly; it is just a matter of our way of looking at it. We can say that someone is taller than another when compared with someone who is shorter. A person can be taller than one person, and shorter than another, but he is not inherently short or tall. Comparisons only exist when there is something to compare to.

Consider if someone is beautiful or ugly. Whatever makes us say someone is beautiful is not independent, permanent, or solid. It is just our view and our attachment. One person may think a woman is beautiful because her eyes are like stars. Another person doesn't like stars, so he thinks the woman is not beautiful. So what is the truth? Where does the definition of beauty and ugliness come from? Where does it arise, and where does it remain? It's all from our manifestations.

It's like watching a magical performance at the theater. When we see a magical performance at the theatre, we see the magicians perform so many amazing things. Watching them, we know that it is simply a performance. It may be an amusing performance, where everyone is entertained and laughs, or it may be very frightening. But none of us has an attachment to it; no one holds it after the performance. We know it's just temporarily there; it's just a magical performance for our entertainment. The moment it's over, we are disconnected from it. Similarly, if we know the real facts about reality, then we see how it's contained within us, within its true state. Therefore, all the great Dzogchen masters from the past lived in this universe, but without any kind of influence from it.

Consider the lotus flower. It grows from the mud, but it is not stained by the mud. When the flower rises above the mud, it's colorful, smooth, full of life, beautiful. Similarly, those great masters were not attached, not attracted, not bounded, not influenced by appearances, because they knew their real condition. They knew the way reality is, the way it appears and remains. Within this understanding, we can live without the influence from them. So, we have to reflect on this introduction, saying that all the surrounding phenomena are simply reflections of our own true state of mind. When we understand the true nature of all things we are dealing with, it will be easy for us to handle them. When we don't understand this true nature, then the appearances affect our life in a positive or negative way.

The purpose of introducing how experience and existing phenomena are connected directly to our own mind is for us to realize and discontinue the grasping and ignorance. Grasping and ignorance put us in illusion. When we realize that everything is rooted in our own mind, then we don't become tied up with illusionary forms and activities based on ignorance. We circle in khorwa because we don't realize the true nature of reality. This introduction is meant to give us an understanding of the real foundation and sources of the true nature of reality.

When we introduce appearances as being a reflection of our own mind, that means the root cause of everything we experience, both joy and suffering, sorrow and happiness, is connected directly with our own self, not with external objects. For example, when we encounter certain conditions that make us angry, we think that our anger is directly connected to the object we encountered, that the object is the source of our anger. In reality, if we think carefully and search precisely and calmly, we will see that reality is not that way. Where does that anger come from? It comes from within us. The object is just a secondary cause, a temporary facility, but it does not produce our anger. That anger is our property. It's not the property of the object that we think is the cause of it. Even when we are away from that particular object, miles from it, in our bedroom, we still carry it, we feel it, we are bothered by it, we are unhappy because of it. We still carry that anger with us, it's within us and not within that object, which may already be a hundred miles away from us. If we carefully think, the object is just an external facility or condition, and the so-called anger, which is strongly bothering us, is really us; it's within us.

When we study this, we may at first understand it, but we don't realize it. Understanding has to change to realization. Understanding is a more academic, intellectual aspect, dealing with the external world. Realization is more about how we feel in the internal world. And we are affected more by our internal world than by the material, external world. When we truly understand and realize that it's the inner dimension that causes our actions, and which is the true source of all our negativity, anger, and five poisons, then there is no reason to get angry. When we realize that our feelings have nothing to do with external conditions or appearances, there is no reason to get angry at the external objects. There is no reason to attach and continually follow those illusionary aspects.

The main point of this teaching is not to say that the world is this way and we cannot do anything about it. The main point is, we have been living our lives to believe that outer appearances and external phenomena are true. In fact, they are illusion. By grasping the outer appearances, we become deluded. We want to break the attachment to the outer appearances.

The reason we are bound to khorwa is because the way we perceive phenomena and the way they exist are two different things. The way we perceive is not necessarily the way they exist, and the way they exist is different from what we perceive. So we have illusionary thoughts that bind us, always distracting us, and we are attracted to objects not as they are, but as we perceive them. Most of the time, we follow reality in the way that we perceive it, not in the way that it actually is. The essence of the practice that is introduced in this session is to change our way of perception, and get closer to reality as it is.

Let's take dream practice as an example. A highly realized dream practitioner realizes the dream state as a dream, experiences dreams as dreams. That practitioner is not distracted or influenced by the dreams, neither the pleasant dreams, nor the frightening ones. The practitioner realizes both of those dreams equally as dreams, with no essence, nothing to attach to. Because of that realization, the practitioner does not attach to the dreams, has no illusions about the dreams. The practitioner has realized the truth and cut off ignorance, the root of suffering. When ignorance is cut off, and distraction and illusion cease, then there is no khorwa. That is called the realization of illusionary form. We realize everything as an illusion, as a dream. Nothing is solid; there is nothing to be attracted or attached to, because everything is just an illusion. When we realize that everything is an illusion, there is no reason to be attracted to anything. Even this realization is an illusion.

When we are riding on a horse, we see a variety of trees, flowers, landscapes, and people along the way. If we are constantly attracted to everything that we think is nice, beautiful, and good, then our whole life will be spent within the limits of that attraction, and we will be unable to free ourselves from those limits. Our energy is projecting and manifesting thoughts and reflections toward the objects we are attracted to, without realizing the true impermanent condition of those objects. Instead, we should reflect on impermanence, on sourcelessness, and on truthlessness. The beautiful objects we see are not solid; there is nothing we can grasp or attach to. We should be like a passing horse rider, who just passes by all the things he sees along the road. If we focus on the true nature of what we experience, then we are moving from khorwa to nyangde.

The essence of introducing appearances and our surrounding existence as manifestation of our mind is like introducing ourselves to how we are deluded. It shows us we are forced into suffering, because we chase illusions. When we genuinely realize the true manifestation aspect of our Nature of Mind, it is like opening our eyes and awakening from the dream state. The introduction of existing phenomena to our own mind, if we understand it, opens our eyes. If we don't understand it, we remain in the dream without realizing that it is a dream, and we keep chasing the illusion.

# Introduction of the Mind as Empty

This is the fifteenth session. In earlier sessions, we talked about introducing phenomena into the mind. Now we will talk about introducing the mind into emptiness.

According to Dzogchen, the mind has three aspects. The first aspect is the essence (*ngo wo*); the second aspect is the nature (*rang zhin*); and the third aspect is energy (*tsal*).

The essence aspect of the Nature of Mind is emptiness. This emptiness is as boundless as the sky, as measureless and deep as the ocean, and as empty as open space.

We introduce the mind as empty, broad, and deep. But what is the mind we are talking about? We are all convinced that our so-called mind exists within us, active, awakened, precise. We feel its presence, but we don't know how it is and where it is. We are all aware that the mind has presence, and this presence is strong and energetic. When somebody makes us happy, we have a strong appreciation inside. When someone is mean to us, we also have a strong reaction inside. Our mind is the key to all of this. Until now, we have talked about mind and all its deeds and connections, but we don't know yet what our mind is, what it looks like, or where it is located.

It's not enough to just believe that our mind is responsible for everything. It's important to search for our mind, discover it, and realize it. We are not searching for something that is not within us. We are trying to identify and discover something that already exists in us. This so-called mind exists equally in all sentient beings. Even the smallest sentient beings are carrying the same mind and the same Nature of Mind. Realizing the mind as it is, we realize the exact person we are searching for. If we don't realize the mind, we are deluded and lost in the midst of khorwa, wrongly identifying things as real and grasping at them. That will put you on one of two paths. We can take the right path that leads to enlightenment, or we can take the wrong path and spend our whole life following illusion in khorwa.

We must realize our face as it is. When we directly find out what our face looks like, when we see it clearly in the mirror, we don't need any further explanation. Our face has never even for a moment been separated from us, but we were not able to see or realize it until we looked in a mirror. When we see our face directly, we don't need anyone to tell us what our face is. The opinions of others don't matter anymore. Their perception is their opinion, but not the reality of our face. We are free from the views of others, because we are aware of each and every aspect of our face directly.

Realizing our mind is very much like realizing our face by ourselves. But what is our mind? What form does it have? What is its shape and color? There is a lot of confusion and misconception about the mind. In the West, many people think the mind is the brain. We are not talking about the brain, or the heart, or the head. We are talking about the mind.

But this mind we are talking about is not a solid object, like a brain or a heart. I can show you a brain or a heart. Instead, we need to experience our mind and gain confidence in that experience of mind. A teacher can only guide us and direct us towards the mind, show us the way to it, tell us how to discover it and what it would be like. But we must make the effort to experience our mind through our practice, or we will not be able to experience the true state of mind by ourselves. It would be like explaining the taste of sweet to people who have never tasted sweets. We need to have a direct experience of our mind, without anyone in between. We need to remove everything that separates us from our mind and from our Nature of Mind. This is an individual experience. When we have our own experience, then the teacher's explanations and descriptions will be clearer and will take us closer and deeper toward the state of our true Nature of Mind.

The text says it is important to realize nakedly, directly, and precisely the natural state of our mind. We have mentioned several times in these sessions that practice is important. Understanding and realization are important, but just remaining in the state of realization is still not the fulfillment. Realization by itself doesn't help us to achieve the ultimate goal. To achieve the goal, realization needs more familiarity, more practice, more force and energy, so that we have experience and confirmation of our realization. We also need to integrate this realization in our everyday activities. First, it is important to realize the Dzogchen view (*tawa*), the view of meditation. Then, we must familiarize ourselves with it by contemplation. This way, we can gradually achieve the final attainment of Dzogchen practice. Achieving the realization is not enough; ultimately, we need to achieve the full strength and perfection of both wisdom and compassion, wisdom and method. We must follow our wisdom and compassion, and use that energy and power to benefit and liberate sentient beings.

All sentient beings have a mind. It's always present, but we have never seen it. It's always there, and still we have never heard it. It's always within us, but we have never tasted it. It's always within us, present and energetic, but we have never felt it. It's always there, although there is no place it came from. It's always there and never goes further. It's always there, but we have not identified it. It's not an object that we can hold or possess as a tangible thing. We cannot see it, cannot identify with our eyes, cannot find it by looking. So where is it? How is it? Have you had this experience?

Realizing our mind makes a big difference in our practice and our lives. Even when we don't know exactly what it is, but we are getting closer to it, it makes a great difference in our day-to-day life. This kind of wisdom and realization has a big impact on the way we deal with circumstances. We are here to practice, so in the time we spend here, it's important to focus on our practice, to understand, experience, know, feel, and identify the true Nature of Mind. Talk and words can lead us in the right direction. But it cannot get us into that state, because that state is beyond words, beyond explanations, and beyond conditions. What helps is to listen, to keep the words that are told to us, and to experiment, search for our mind, and discover it.

Traditionally, in Tibet, lamas would keep a student for a few weeks or months or even a year, just practicing and searching to discover his true Nature of Mind by his own practice. The teacher would give some instruction, then give his student a time for practice. The student would report after a week, a month, three months, or a year, depending on the capacity of the practitioner and the way in which the teacher was introducing the Nature of Mind. Some teachers are very strict and let the student put a lot of effort in finding it. After the specified time, the student goes to the teacher, individually, because these experiences are not public, but between the teacher and the student. Not everyone has the same level of understanding and experience, and the teacher needs to clarify or instruct the student according to the student's level of understanding or discovery.

We must do our best, according to our circumstances, to look into ourselves and try to search for, and discover, our mind. We need to meditate and practice, because we are talking about something that is on the individual level of experience. That experience is not something we all share as a view; it's not something we share in discussion. Rather, it has to arise in our own experience and personal feeling. Some students, because of their karmic connections from the past, may only need a simple direction to awaken. Others need a lot of effort and support, both from their side and from the teacher's side.

When we go within ourselves, there are completely new worlds that we may see and experience. Within the appearances of endlessly arising thoughts, there still is some clear awakened presence that we may identify. The experience may make sense to us or not. We may be able to communicate it or not. But expressing it in words doesn't mean that the mind has been introduced directly. We must continue our practice to have the clear, direct, naked experience of our mind.

Our mind is not visible as an object, but it's energetically present within us. We all agree that it's present, but we have different ways of identifying and conceptualizing our mind. Generally, when we think about our mind, it's clear that it is beyond limits and boundaries and measurements. But how do we discover it?

According to the view of the Middle Way (Madhyamaka), which is the highest view of dho, the Nature of Mind is emptiness. And according to this Middle Way view, we search for our mind by using reason and philosophy. When we search everywhere for our mind and find nothing solid, dho says this establishes a finding—that this "nothing" is the Nature of Mind. The text explains that the dho view of emptiness is, "not finding a solid, inherent mind," which means it is free from the eight mental fabrications. Our internal dualistic thought decided that the "nothing" it found is the Nature of Mind. Dho says that when someone remains in that state, he remains in the Nature of Mind, without going beyond it, bound by this thought.

The Dzogchen view of emptiness is different. Dzogchen recognizes that emptiness is an aspect of one quality of the Nature of Mind. We don't use our thoughts to put emptiness into the Nature of Mind. We find that emptiness is an inherently existing quality of the Nature of Mind. The Dzogchen view is that the Nature of Mind is not something bound by thoughts or names. The Nature of Mind is not something we find. The Dzogchen view is that both our mind and its nature have always been with us. It's just a matter of discovering our mind and its nature. Our true Nature of Mind is inside us. If we realize it, truly from the inside, then we cut the root of khorwa. If we don't realize it, we remain in khorwa. The difference is in realizing and not realizing, discovering and not discovering. That is all.

This seems simple. Just realize and discover. Some of the Dzogchen texts make it sound very simple and easy to understand and realize the natural state of mind. The texts often tell us to be present the way it is, without touching or moving anything, just leave it as it is, and everything will be liberated by itself. Other Dzogchen texts tell us that if we do too much, we could easily sink back into the ocean of khorwa. If we do too much and are too active, we could get lost. So, just leave everything as it is. These words are easy to say and a welcome idea to practitioners who are tired of doing too much. How can Dzogchen be the highest form of teaching if it is the easiest—if we don't have to do anything? This does not mean that actively doing something makes us realize our

Nature of Mind, because the Nature of Mind is beyond action, beyond doing.

Our Nature of Mind has never been hidden from us. It's always present. It's always with us and has never been separated from us. Our dualistic mind thinks it's something to achieve. The dualistic mind perceives it in categories of two different objects, of subject and object. Our dualistic mind thinks that when it has to identify and discover something, there should be something else to discover, and someone who discovers it. So, the one who discovers, and the objects being discovered, look like two different objects. We think these are two solid parts, two solid forms, like subject and object, until somebody says that this is not the way it is.

When the Dzogchen texts tell us to do nothing and leave everything as it is, they mean we should not project anything by our own thoughts, from our dualistic point of view. We should not make judgments or definitions. We shouldn't try to create the natural state of mind ourselves. Sometimes, we decide to sit and meditate on the natural state of mind. We close our eyes. Sometimes, we even don't realize whether we are in the state of dullness or whether we are awakened; we are unclear and lazy, relaxed. But we think we are in the natural state of mind. Sometimes, we meditate and lose focus, just actively enjoying the moment, and then a thought arises, "This must be the Nature of Mind." This is an example of how we make our own definitions and limitations. We instruct ourselves this way, we try to be this way, and we think this is the meditation on the Nature of Mind. We must be careful not to do this.

One time, I spoke with a man about his personal experience of meditation. He explained to me that he enjoys his meditation. He wasn't asking for my advice or help. He was rather reporting to me his experience; he just wanted me to know what he is meditating. He explained that every time he meditates, after some moment he begins to fly in the sky, and he abides within the space of the sky, perfectly enjoying this experience. He said that he thinks this is his natural state of mind. This was his own way of identifying the natural state of mind. And he didn't want to lose that experience. He told me that he doesn't want to change it, so he doesn't want me to explain whether I think this is right or not. He just wanted to tell me how happy he is. What could I say? I just wished him good luck. But really, he was just wasting his time. That wasn't his Nature of Mind, it was his dualistic thoughts and mental fabrication tricking him.

There are limitless experiences we can have in our meditation. Sometimes people are confused, think that these experiences are the realization of the Nature of Mind, and waste their time following them. It's very important to be very precise and correct when we talk about the natural state of mind. If we are wrong in this view, then our meditation is wrong, our experience will be wrong, the results will be wrong, and we will waste a lot of time and end up in the wrong place. When we read Dzogchen texts, we don't read a lot of new things. The texts give explanations, describe ways to meditate, and tell us how to discover the natural state of mind. We should follow the instructions of these texts. That's what is essential. If we try to find the Nature of Mind in another way, it's like following a wrong map, and we will not reach our true destination. To reach the right place at the right time and in the right way, it's important to discover everything properly, perfectly, and correctly.

It is important to be precise, because we are discussing the mind itself. It is boundless and limitless. Therefore, we say it's completely open. It encompasses everything, and at the same time it's so narrow that there is no space. It's so wide that it has no end, because everything can fit into it: the whole universe, all of khorwa, and nyangde; but it is also so narrow that nobody except you can fit in it. I am not talking about the Nature of Mind. I'm talking about the mind. We say that the mind has such a great capacity that it can hold everything, and yet it's so narrow it can only fit ourselves. We call it boundless and matchless, and say it has no end of capacity. All the perfect qualities are in it, and all sorrow and suffering are also within it. That's the mind I'm talking about.

Now, we have agreed on what we are talking about; but when we agree on something, who is agreeing? Our body is not saying anything. Our mouth is not saying anything by itself, it only expresses what someone else tells it to express. But who is governing all of this? Who is telling us to agree and not agree, to be happy and not happy? Who is responsible? Who is instructing us? There is someone there. We do what this someone tells us. Our body acts according to orders given by somebody. But who gives the orders? The mind gives the orders. When the mind gives an order, our body accepts it without any choice, and we just do it. When our mind doesn't agree on something, we will not move, because we are not told to do so. We have to find that mind, we have to discover it, realize it, and identify it; because it is the source of all experiences in our daily life.

When we don't realize that appearances are only manifestations of our own mind, then we are deluded. And when we are deluded, we separate reality into two solid categories. Every fact has a real source, real conditions, real qualities. It's important to know them, because only then we can find the solutions.

All problems are dependent on our inner conditions, not external conditions. The condition and source of our suffering is ignorance. Suffering means unhappiness. Suffering is a result of being in khorwa. Individual khorwa, individual ignorance, our individual inner problems, are connected directly to our inside. In the last session, we discussed the realization of the connection of our inner reflections and existing phenomena that surround us. If we realize that true source, it will automatically disconnect the illusion between our inner conditions and our external, surrounding conditions.

When we talk about our true inside, we mean our mind. That mind can make all the difference. It can make everything peaceful, sound, healthy, and happy when it is properly and truly realized and understood. But also, it makes everything horrible and full of misery when it is not realized, when it's deluded and distracted by ignorance and by poisons. It's our responsibility to reflect on our mind and on our Nature of Mind, to go into it and discover it.

The mind itself has no shape. Even though it exists, no one has been able to measure it. No one has found it to be solid as we see it, as we judge it to be. The time of its birth has never been found; no one has found its source. It's not born from anything; it never has ceased to continue; it's always present, always functioning. But it has no form that we can identify as an object, even though we try.

After all of this searching and not finding anything solid and independent that we can identify as the mind, we begin to think the mind doesn't exist. That is not the case; it does exist. We feel it clearly. When I talk to you, you listen and respond. Who responds? Who is present here? Who thinks about these questions I am asking? That is the presence. It has no inner or outer boundary. It's not created by Sanggye, and it will not be destroyed by the most harmful person. It exists in every being without distinguishing; each and every being holds that quality. Our experience in every moment, peaceful and wrathful, happy and sorrowful, good and bad, is directly connected to it. All the perfect qualities of enlightenment are perfected within it. All the varieties of visionary experiences are manifested from it. No existence exists independently; it's continuously, spontaneously manifesting. But manifestation and its true nature of equanimity are unified. It has no description, it's beyond expression, beyond dualistic thoughts. It means that it's beyond reach of our dualistic thought. When we realize rigpa, it's not a dualistic thought, but a special awareness that directly and nakedly recognizes the natural state of mind. This awareness is rigpa; it's not a dualistic thought by which we hold the awareness.

What I have given you is a rough description. As I mentioned earlier, the natural state of mind is beyond description. Words cannot give us the naked introduction to this experience. All of its qualities are perfect, because no one has put any special effort to gain the perfect qualities of enlightenment. The moment we achieve enlightenment is the same moment everything is perfected within this state. All the perfect qualities of enlightenment come from within it, not from outside. Waves and energy manifesting from the ocean are within the ocean, they are not separate from it. Strong waves of the ocean can destroy things. The ocean has the capacity to destroy; it has a capacity to give birth; it has great capacity to affect phenomena. But no matter what form its effects take on, they are still the energy and manifestation of the ocean.

All our qualities, our suffering and our positive qualities, are manifested by our mind. If these qualities were something we received from the outside, something we planned to get, we would not choose unhappiness. No one plans to be unhappy and to suffer. If it were in our power to plan, to make a choice, who would choose unhappiness? This shows that happiness and unhappiness are not within our power. They are simply the way our mind perceives phenomena. Because these are directly rooted in our true Nature of Mind, all these qualities may arise within the mind itself. We can overcome khorwa simply by realizing it as it is, without making any effort to avoid or remove suffering or negativity. Simply discovering the natural state is enough, and it makes everything perfect.

We may wonder: "If everything is a manifestation of our own mind, do we have to make all this effort and practice?" Everything is contained in the natural state. But if we don't realize this, then we fall into khorwa due to our illusions. Sometimes we do some awful thing without even necessarily noticing it, until somebody tells us we are doing a bad thing, or until very late, when we realize it's not good. But until then, we feel everything is OK, everything we do is good, reasonable, and based on good judgment. It's not because of wrong intentions but because of a lack of understanding—because we don't realize the nature of phenomena as they are. So, the moment we realize this state, we stop the negativities. When we realize, either by introduction from someone else or by our own knowledge and wisdom, that we are doing wrong, we realize our behavior as not good, and we begin to change; we begin to transform. The moment we realize it, the moment we stop the negative perception, we begin to awaken, to see things as they are. We begin to change. The moment we discover it's not right, we begin to change.

The fact that we have positive and negative manifestations doesn't mean that we store all of them. Instead, we already have a bank deposit of karmic traces. When the right conditions arise, a manifestation based on one of these karmic traces may appear. That recognition can be achieved in this lifetime or in the state of the bardo, depending on the capacity of the individual practitioner. But, as long as we have that capacity of understanding and experience of that understanding, then at the same time, when we realize it, we discontinue that particular actions. That is how our decisions can make a difference and are connected to our own mind.

We have seen that our mind is directly connected with all existing phenomena, with all the conditions of happiness and sorrow, with the two major paths of khorwa and nyangde. Both suffering and joy, happiness and unhappiness, perfection and illusion, are within that state. Our mind itself in neither of these, neither khorwa nor nyangde, neither happiness nor sorrow. It only appears as suffering or happiness when we perceive it that way. When we perceive with clear realization, we get happiness. When we perceive with illusions, we get sorrow and suffering. And we are the one who controls which way we will perceive.

And as we've already discussed, understanding is not enough. We have to know the view, but then we have to practice it, and then we have to realize it and achieve it. If we think about this state, if we reflect on it carefully, it will make some difference for us, even though we may not discover it as close and direct as it is. But there will be something that makes sense for us, so it's important to reflect on it.

## Introduction of the Ku Sum – the Three Enlightened Bodies

As we have seen, the mind is connected with everything. Everything reflects from within it. What we see, how we see it, how long it remains there, what remains there, where it comes from, and where it goes, all reflects from the mind.

In Bön, we talk about three bodies of enlightenment. These three are *bönku*, *dzogku* and *tulku*, and together they are referred to as *ku sum* ("three enlightened bodies"). *Bönku* is represented by Kuntu Zangpo, *dzogku* is represented by Shenlha Ökar, and *tulku* is represented by Tonpa Shenrab. The first one, *bönku*, is the primordial state, the Primordial Sanggye. The second is *dzogku*, the body of perfection, also known as Sanggye of Compassion. The third one is known as Tulku Tonpa Shenrab, the body of manifestation.

When we achieve the true natural state of mind and discover it, when we reach some level of recognition and experience in a practical way, the empty aspect of nature is known as Bönku. Since it is empty, it's depicted as naked; it has no form. Bönku Kuntu Zangpo is the true aspect of the nature of emptiness.

We have discussed that, according to Dzogchen, the mind has three aspects. The first aspect is the essence (*ngo wo*); the second aspect is the nature (*rang zhin*); and the third aspect is the energy (*tsal*).

The first aspect, the essence aspect, is emptiness. When we realize emptiness as the true Nature of Mind itself, we achieve the recognition of the true nature of Bönku Kuntu Zangpo, the nature of the primordial state.

The second aspect, the nature aspect, is clarity. This is the aspect of *dzogku*, meaning "all-perfected." The *dzogku* is depicted as Shenlha Ökar, a fully clothed form of white light, adorned with thirteen peaceful ornaments. As in the name *Dzogchen*, also here, *dzog* means "perfection." *Dzogku* means that all qualities of enlightenment are perfected, no quality is lacking, and everything is within this body of light. Why do we say that everything is perfected in it? This is the second aspect of the Nature of Mind, which is clarity. That clarity makes everything appear as forms, as objects.

Therefore, Shenlha Ökar is depicted as having a costume, ornaments, and colors, although in reality, his form is not a material object; it is a form of light. He is depicted in this way symbolically, to make it easier for us sentient beings to understand. Without seeing those aspects, we wouldn't be able to imagine it; our inner child wouldn't be able to understand what we are talking about. The clarity aspect of our mind is that the mind is clear; it has no darkness. It's completely enlightened and bright, completely aware of everything, without any kind of delusion or distraction.

The third aspect, the energy aspect, is manifestation. Sanggye Tonpa Shenrab, and any other of the manifested Sanggye, represents this third aspect of the mind. Symbolically, it means that this energy keeps flourishing, growing, like Sanggye Tonpa Shenrab, who represents all the enlightened beings, and who appeared as a teacher to guide us, teach us, and liberate us.

These three aspects of enlightenment, three bodies of light, are not separate from us. These three aspects of enlightenment are within us; they are aspects of our own mind. According to our recognition and achievement, we can realize the Sanggye within us. Therefore, we say that the Sanggye is within us, and khorwa is within us. When we see these three aspects as they are, we achieve enlightenment. When we don't see them as they are, we become deluded and we begin to circle in khorwa. That is how it is. That's how close and how far we are from our own true qualities. We are so close, because all these three aspects of enlightenment are within us. They are parts of our own mind. But they are so far, because we are still circling, life after life, and it still seems that we are still far away from achieving our ultimate goal. We are circling in khorwa, and illusion is pushing us away from our true nature.

Sometimes, in dreams and in deep sleep, when we are not fully awake but also not deeply asleep, we may perceive or project a shadow or image of a movement, or we may blink our eyes. This causes us to awaken and jump up, because we confuse the image or projection for reality. We follow our illusions, and they affect us. We scare ourselves and put ourselves in great trouble, because of our own illusions. Because we don't know it's an illusion, we think it is solid and true. We should reflect on the main difficulty, the main problem we have to deal with in our daily life. Is it our anger, is it our hatred, is it our jealousy, our pride, our ignorance? What is the most difficult thing we have to deal with in our day-to-day life? Reflect on how it affects us. Why is it so hard? How do we realize that it is hard for us? We should reflect on all these aspects. What will we find? Does it make sense or not? Again, whether it makes sense or not is connected to us. Who finds sense in it? Who doesn't find sense in it? When we realize something is an illusion, there is no reason why we should chase after it as if it were solid and real.

As we have discussed, the third aspect of the mind, the energy aspect, is manifestation. Because of this third aspect of the mind, all phenomena spontaneously arise from the Nature of Mind. All visual appearances, both internal and external, arise in the same context. They have no solid form—no independent source or stability. They arise spontaneously, in their own way, not in the way we expect them to, not in the way someone forces them, but in their own way. Visual appearances arise whether we have our eyes open or closed. Normally, when we see things with our eyes open, we think they are more solid and real, and when we experience appearances with closed eyes, we think of them as illusions, as only thoughts. In the Dzogchen view, it doesn't make any difference whether we experience these appearances with our eyes open or closed. If we think and analyze carefully, both conditions are the same.

Consider the appearances that arise when our eyes are closed. When we meditate, our eyes are closed. Even with our eyes closed, we still have inner appearances that arise continuously. The arising is not solid, has no inherent existence. It doesn't appear from its own side, by its own efforts; it appears because of our mind, from inside us. This "mind" we are talking about is the base of all appearances, both inner and outer. We view these appearances as distractions to our meditation, something to be avoided.

Now, consider the experiences we encounter in our day-to-day life. Many experiences arise. Sometimes we are satisfied and happy, sometimes we are disappointed and unhappy. These experiences also arise from within our mind, which is the base of appearances. When we meditate, we view these arisings as a distraction. In our daily life, we see these same arisings as part of our life, as difficulties or problems to be dealt with. And then we expend our efforts to solve these difficulties and problems.

It is like looking at water in a pond. When the water is still and calm, we can see the bottom through it. When the water is stirred and mud arises, we cannot see the bottom clearly. Both the mud and the clear water are present in the pond. The water is inherently clear.

The mud doesn't come from somewhere else; it arises from inside the pond, but we don't see it until we stir the water. The difference arises when we either stir the water, or when we allow it to settle. From the Dzogchen view, from the aspect of the true nature of our mind, the water is neither clear nor disturbed. It always remains the same. But it appears to be different. When arisings are distracting us in meditation, we see them as more active, we concentrate on that aspect, we focus on it, and that's why we clearly see the distractions.

When we take a broader view, we see that all appearances, both the appearances of khorwa and of nyangde, arise from inside us in the same way. All our experiences, the experience of unhappiness, the experience of happiness, the experience of ignorance, and the experience of realization and wisdom, arise from inside. Like our example of the pond, the mud doesn't come from outside, it arises from within the pond. All our experiences come from the mind's base, which is the kunzhi, the base of all. We have to realize and notice that both external and internal appearances arise from our mind in the same way.

Having this realization is not enough. We must apply it in our daily life.

The text tells us that there are three important aspects: contemplating the natural state; abiding in that state; and changing or transforming our distracted thoughts and illusion into clarity and wisdom. In the Dzogchen view, this transformation occurs naturally as a result of contemplation; it is not something we force.

The process of meditation is really two steps. First, we must understand what we are going to meditate. The Tibetan word *gom* is translated as "meditate," but it literally means "to become familiar" with something, to train ourselves to get familiar with the subject of our meditation. Most of us have no difficulty recalling our mother's face. Immediately, when we think about our mother, we have a clear picture of her. It is same with a person whom we love very much. Immediately, when we start talking about that person, a clear picture of his or her face comes to our mind without any difficulty or effort. We are very familiar with that face, because we often see their face and think about them. We are a well-trained practitioner of that face. This is real familiarity. This is *gom*.

If we want to mediate on something, we must have a clear understanding of it. We must become familiar with it. If we don't have a clear understanding and familiarity, even though we may think we are meditating, we are really just wasting our time.

When we are familiar (through *gom*) with a particular thing, then we contemplate it. The Tibetan name for contemplation is *nyam zhak*. *Nyam* means remaining in deep silence, peace, and equanimity, without follow to the right or left, without boundaries, without distinguishing. *Zhak* means leaving it, being within it. We should be with the object of meditation the way it is, without modifying it, without any fabrication by our thoughts. We should just be with it as it is, and we should leave it in that state. This is called contemplation. In contemplation, we remain where we are, within ourselves, inseparable from our state of being. Whether we are contemplating the natural state of mind according to Dzogchen, or we are contemplating the natural state of mind according to dho, or we are contemplating compassion or semkyed, contemplation means maintaining our focus, our concentration, and remaining in it. We should continue without any distractions, without letting any arising thoughts disturb our contemplation. And as long as we can stay in that contemplation, we call it "resting within."

The purpose of our daily life is not just meditation. We can meditate only for an hour or two, but what happens after that? Our day has 24 hours. How many hours can we meditate? Two, three, four hours? What about the rest of time? If, right after our meditation period, we go back to being the same as we were, then we are again completely mixed up in khorwa. So, in order to benefit our daily life, we need to contemplate, but that contemplation has to be practiced until we can integrate it with our daily life. The first step is to be mindful, to control our concentration, and to try to remain fully present. When we are well-trained and well-experienced, and we know clearly how to meditate, then we apply it in our daily life.

The next point in the text deals with beginning meditation and dismissing meditation. This is a part of the growth of our meditation practice. It is important to have a good level of experience and familiarity with meditation, so that when we want to meditate, we can begin our meditation without any special effort, without any preparation. Similarly, we should be able to release our meditation when we want. We should be able to meditate the moment we think about meditating; and the moment we think about releasing, we should be able to release without any hesitation. When we can do this, we can choose any time or place to mediate: a noisy bus, a train station, a stadium.

We need to practice to get to that level. At our present stage, we can meditate more easily when everything is peaceful and calm, no one is around us, no dogs barking, no telephones ringing. It's like we are hiding from reality. We try to find a more comfortable position to meditate, but on the other hand, we are trying to hide from what we cannot hide from; we try to run away from what we cannot run away from. Momentary external calmness facilitates a sense of so-called peace within us. But when we develop peace from inside, then we won't have to run away from anything. We can be anywhere and be happy and peaceful.

We have to learn a second phase of meditation. We can develop it gradually. To start, when we are meditating and our concentration is still within the state of meditation, we can try to move our hand without disturbing our meditation. If we are able to do this, then to develop further, we should try to stand up and move around a little bit, still trying to remain in contemplation, in the state of realization. When we gradually develop in that way, we can activate our daily routines and see how much we can go into them while keeping our meditation. Then both day-to-day life and practice will go together.

When we are able to remain in this state of meditation in our active life, then every moment of our day is not separated from our practice, and none of our activities are separated from it. Each and every moment, as long as we are within those circumstances, we are practicing. Although we are taking care of our day-to-day life and businesses, we still are in practice. It is similar to driving. An experienced driver can drive while carrying on a conversation or listening to music. In the same way, we can continuously carry on our normal activities while we are in the state of awakened, energetic realization.

The third stage is continuation in practice. When we remain in continuation of practice, every moment is practice. Dzogchen masters weren't people who always spent their lives in caves, sitting in meditation position. They practiced on retreats at certain times, for a while, but then they were also active in society. They generated the aspiration to benefit people by their wisdom and compassion, and to guide and lead people, so they had to be part of society. Every moment, wherever they were, they were not separate from their inner wisdom. Of course, to reach that level, we need strong practice, time, good fortune, cultivation of merit, and so on. But when our inner strength of recognition and realization is at such a level, then even if we physically are a child our wisdom can benefit others.

There is a story about Shen Nyima Gyaltsen (born 1357), a well-known great Bönpo master from the Shen lineage of Tonpa Shenrab. He lived at the time of Nyammed Sherab Gyaltsen, in the fourteenth century. He is known as a real, direct emanation of the deity of Ma Gyu in the ngag tradition. When he was about seven or eight years old, an elder person from a nomad family died, and the family members gave to him an offering of many sheep. In our tradition, when someone dies, people go to high lamas whom they trust and with whom they have a connection. They make offerings of sheep, horses, yaks, or any wealth, and request the lama to perform a *phowa* or otherwise enlighten the deceased person, performing some ritual or ceremony to free that person from suffering of khorwa. When the family gave all those sheep to Shen Nyima Gyaltsen, his treasurer, without his knowledge, ordered that the sheep be sold. The nomads who offered those sheep were disappointed and unhappy, because that meant the sheep would be slaughtered for their meat. They regretted their decision to come there. They had expected to perform a virtuous ceremony for their deceased family member, but instead they helped in a negative deed of killing the sheep for meat. Even though Shen Nyima Gyaltsen was very young, he had great wisdom, and by his wisdom he knew their thoughts and realized that they had the wrong view towards him and his deeds. Shen Nyima Gyaltsen ordered his men to collect all the slaughtered sheep heads in one place, on the veranda of his house. He came from his personal chapel to the veranda, performed prayers, ceremony, and *phowa*. Then, he transformed all the sheep heads in front of them and dissolved them into rainbow light.

My main purpose for telling this story is so you know that for someone that reaches a high level of realization and understanding, all phenomena of khorwa and nyangde are inseparable as one essence. There is no such thing as "upper" or "lower," nothing is "good" or "bad," nothing is separated, everything is integrated, and everything is within the quality of perfection. There is no khorwa or nyangde separately existing within it. There is no duality. Everything is unified into oneness.

From our ordinary view, for us non-realized common people, it's very important what someone looks like, how he presents himself, and how he acts. We think, "He is so wise; he is so great," because of the way he looks. This view is very strong within us. But this is an illusion. When we look at things the way they are, these external appearances are not real in the way we think.

Dzogchen says that the true quality of the natural state of mind is not distracted by suffering and miseries, and neither is it modified by enlightenment. Neither of those can affect the natural state of mind, because it is beyond them. Once we are in the natural state of mind, then everything is perfect, positive, and correct. Our realization, and the observation of our mind, makes that difference. It depends on our level and stability of insight. The natural state of mind is very well-known and famous, but it's not a visible object that everybody can see. Rather, we must realize it is an inseparable aspect of our own mind.

The natural state is pure from primordial time. Everything is spontaneously perfect within it. It's pure and perfect from beginningless time. There are no obscurations, no distractions in it. It's pure from the beginning. It never had any faults. It has always been in the pure state. It's spontaneously perfect, it's perfect without any effort, everything is already included within it, and everything is perfect there. It is effortless, it doesn't require any effort or conditions, and everything is spontaneously perfected within it. Like the sun, which has perfect brightness, light, rays, and heat, everything is perfect within it. Nobody has to make the sun brighter, more beautiful, or hotter. Nobody could do this, and nobody has done it. The perfection of the natural state is spontaneous. Therefore, we say that it is perfect within itself.

*Kunzhi jang chub kyi sem* is the base of all, which connects khorwa and nyangde. It means that everything is connected within the base; everything is reflected from the base. It doesn't mean that it's created or planted, but everything arises spontaneously as reflections of that state. And this state also has a quality of inseparability. It is like a single point. *Nelug thigle nyagchig* is the single-pointed nature of all phenomena; it's highest, simple, and single. Because everything is spontaneously perfected within it, the natural state of our mind is also perfected with these three aspects of the enlightened bodies. How do we see it? How do we realize it? Where does it exist? How does it exist? We are looking for it— searching for it. It's the famous, so-called natural state of mind. Where does it exist? What does it look like?

We should concentrate and try to be within the true state of the Nature of Mind, without allowing ourselves to be distracted by any kind of active appearances, disturbances, or distractions. At that moment, feeling energetic presence and clarity, with full awareness, we should remain in that state, in our mind, within ourselves. When we try to be still, at certain times we will experience a state that is beyond expression, beyond our ability to comment, beyond our ability to explain. Something is present and clear. That inner state is the unity of clarity and emptiness. This "emptiness" is not "nothingness." Instead, it is spacious and filled with energetic presence. This is rigpa, the natural state of mind. It's this rigpa we have been talking about.

Once we discover this rigpa, we must be careful not to chase after it or grasp at it. If we attempt to grasp or hold on to rigpa, we become attached to it, and we fall into emotion. If we remain in rigpa without grasping, without holding, without chasing after it, then we are really within the state of rigpa.

Rigpa has been with us from the time we were born. We are still far away from it only because we haven't yet opened the inner wisdom, the inner eye through which we can discover it. If we keep looking beyond ourselves, we won't find anything, not in this life or in our next lives. We will not find anything else outside of ourselves. Within the state of rigpa, all the qualities of the three bodies are perfected. When we realize the true nature of all phenomena, we achieve enlightenment.

Our initial realization of the true nature of phenomena lasts just for a moment. As we continue our practice, this realization extends longer and becomes stronger. Gradually, it becomes possible to achieve the body of light, the rainbow body. When we achieve the body of light, we can transform ourselves into light. This is not performing a miracle; this is integrating ourselves into the light that is our origin.

## Rainbow Body

Dzogchen is unique among Bön and Nyingma Buddhist philosophies, because Dzogchen holds that we can attain enlightenment in one lifetime. There are many stories of Dzogchen masters attaining rainbow body.

Let's discuss rainbow body further. Generally, we talk about the importance of the five elements—the five inner elements and the five outer elements. These elements are associated with five colors, one color for each element. All sentient beings are a composition of the five elements. We see these elements as being concrete, but in essence, they have no inherent existence. They arise from light and return to light. When we die, the earth element is the first to dissolve. When the earth element dissolves, all our inner visions take on a yellowish color and appear as yellowish light. The earth element gradually dissolves into water, water dissolves into fire, fire dissolves into air, and air dissolves into space. At the end, everything dissolves and integrates with its origin, the base of all, *kunzhi jang chub kyi sem*.

At the end, when our inner breath stops, our consciousness appears for a brief moment, bright and sparkling, in the middle of our forehead, in the form of a collection of five colored light. This is the critical moment just before entering the bardo. For ordinary people, the light transforms and disappears, and the person goes through the process of the bardo. But highly realized beings are able to realize that the bright light appearing at the forehead is their rigpa. When they realize this, they go straight to enlightenment and do not go through the process of the bardo.

There are certain signs that can be seen in a person who is about to attain rainbow body. Their bodies begin to lose their substance and become insubstantial. The first sign is, when they go to tie a rope or sash around their waist, the rope will fall away, knotted only to itself. The second sign is that they will have no karmic dreams, i.e. no illusion or emotional dreams. The third sign is that they will not cast a shadow when they stand in the sun, nor leave any footprints when they walk in the sand. The fourth sign is that they will not have any lice or other insects in their hair or on their bodies.

These signs mean they are highly realized beings, even though they show themselves to us ordinary people. They talk, sometimes they show some impatience, sometimes they may show some anger, but it's only being shown for us. They have become fully integrated with their inner true state. Therefore, the rope just knots itself, they leave no shadow, no footprints, etc. There are a lot of symptoms that indicate that a master will achieve the body of light. While these are visible signs, there are also inner blessings and miracles that are beyond our comprehension.

The main point of these teachings is that everything depends very much on how we perceive it. We are able to train our mind to become authoritative and powerful, never far from the Nature of Mind. No matter what our actions look like, our being is always in the state of its true nature.

## Stories of Yogis

We speak about the mind, rigpa, and controlling our perception of the world. This can be abstract at times. In Tibetan, we have many biographies of great yogis who did wonderful things while in the natural state of mind. These stories can bring this abstract discussion to life and encourage us to practice. I will mention two of these stories here.

Once, one of the great masters of the A-tri lineage was introducing the natural state of mind to his student. His disciple was very capable, but his practice was not very consistent and was frequently interrupted. This is because in Tibet at that time, practitioners often lived with their teachers, often in remote areas. The practitioners would have to leave the teachers from time to time to go to distant villages to beg for food. When they got some food, they could come back and practice for two or three months, and when they ran out of food, then they had to go begging for food again. For this reason, the development of their practice was unstable. The student was disappointed, and he went to complain to his teacher. He told him that he had some meditation experiences when he was with him, but then he had to go begging and lost his practice again. The teacher told him that there is a way to regain his practice—that he can introduce him to the way to bring his practice back, so he shouldn't worry.

In that region, it is wet in the summer, and the grass gets wet and very slippery. The master invited the student for a walk. This student's name was Togden Gomchen Barwa. The lama took him to a slippery meadow and asked him to run down the meadow and jump. Gomchen Barwa did this and ran down, but because it was wet, he slipped and fell badly. And the fall caused him to have an awakening; he realized the natural state of mind. From then on, he never lost the realization of the natural state of mind.

One of the great masters, Togden Namkha Yungdrung, who lived in the time of Shen Nyima Gyaltsen, was once invited with him to perform a *phowa* ritual for a nomad, who recently died. Shen Nyima Gyaltsen was a little bit younger than Togden Namkha Yungdrung. Togden was older and very well known. *Togden* is a title of great yogis, *naljorpas*. It literally means, "the holder of great wisdom of realization." He was always within the wisdom of realization. Never, for a single moment, was he away from that realization. When they came to perform *phowa*, Togden, as the elder, was sitting at the head of the opposite row from where Shen Nyima Gyaltsen sat. Shen Nyima Gyaltsen, although he was very famous, was the younger, so he was sitting opposite Togden.

When they were doing the death rituals, before Shen Nyima Gyaltsen performed the *phowa*, Togden Namkha Yungdrung hid the consciousness of the dead person under the offering plate with the *torma*. He wanted to see whether the famous Shen Nyima Gyaltsen really had the capability to find the hidden consciousness of the dead person. Shen Nyima Gyaltsen realized that Togden had hidden the consciousness of that person. He thought, "As long as the consciousness is there, there's no need to bring it back and forth, it's fine to leave it where it is." Togden Rinpoche saw that the consciousness stayed in the same place, and he thought that Shen Nyima Gyaltsen didn't realize that it was hidden or couldn't find it, so he wouldn't be able to transform it. When the time came to transfer the consciousness, Shen Nyima Gyaltsen made the "PHÄT" sound of transformation. Normally, the "PHÄT" sound causes the consciousness to rise up in the internal channel and transfer out of the body. This time, the transfer caused the consciousness to blow the plate up in the air as it transferred. Togden Namhka Yungdrung immediately realized the boy's capacity and high realization at such a young age. To show his appreciation, Togden Namkha Yungdrung picked up a handful of sand, transformed it into gold, and offered it to Shen Nyima Gyaltsen.

What do we learn from this story? This story tells us that the way we appear externally is not important; it's our inside that matters. Material objects that we see are not the truth. The truth is that through our inner capacity we can authoritatively transform objects. Togden brought a handful of sand and transformed it into gold. Sand is not gold; gold is not sand. He took sand, but through his inner capacity of realization, through the stability of his inner realization, he could focus on it and transform it. If the capacity of our inner mind has strength of focus, and also has stable realization of the nature of all phenomena as they are, then objects become the way we present them. That means that there is no material object that is unchangeable. Material objects are unstable and changeable. When someone is a highly realized being, they understand that everything can be changed and transformed. A handful of sand can be transformed into a handful of gold.

Another important lesson from this story is that we cannot always judge a person by their behavior and outlook, because the inner capacity of everyone is beyond the judgment of our ordinary mind. Even Togden Rinpoche did not judge; he checked whether Shen Nyima Gyaltsen had the capacity to transform the consciousness of the dead person. We cannot judge a person according to the way they act, because inner wisdom is not visible. We can see the outer beauty of the tiger's skin, but we cannot see the human's inner beauty. So, we should not judge another's qualities and level of realization based on our own limited understanding and imperfect judgment.

# Conclusion

In this book, I have covered the full teaching of the essence of Dzogchen. I have started from the beginning of developing compassion, loving-kindness, equanimity and the generation of the mind of enlightenment, and the rest of the very important preliminary practices. Then, I moved on to *trekchöd, thögyal,* and beyond. I have explained these things as clearly as I can.

I urge you to read this book many times, reflect on it, experience it internally, and let it make a difference in the way you think and act in everyday life in khorwa. Then, liberate all emotions and karmic defilements in the Dzogchen state of freedom from this cyclic world. Live in absolute freedom from the bounds of the cyclic world, and rest forever in great joy and happiness.

The purpose of doing this, the purpose of all Bön, is to benefit all sentient beings. I especially want this book to benefit serious practitioners seeking to deepen their own realization and understanding of the truth of all phenomena, and implement it in their daily lives. In this way, they may be of service to all sentient beings, and at the same time, both make this present life meaningful and ultimately achieve the state of Dzogchen liberation.

I dedicate any merit and positive qualities gained from this work to peace in the world and for the long life of all great teachers. May this serve to fulfill any unfulfilled wish of the late His Holiness, the 33rd sMenri Trizin, former Spiritual Head of Bön, with blessings and prayers for all good on earth.

# Appendix

# About Latri Nyima Dakpa Rinpoche

Latri Khenpo Geshe Nyima Dakpa Rinpoche is a senior geshe at sMenri Monastery in Dolanji, India. Rinpoche is the lineage holder and abbot of Latri Monastery in the Kham region of eastern Tibet. Rinpoche received his geshe degree (equivalent to a Ph.D. in the West) in 1987 from the Bön Dialectic School at sMenri Monastery in Dolanji, India. He is officially enthroned and recognized by the 33rd sMenri Trizin as a Rinpoche at sMenri Monastery.

Rinpoche's early education came from his father, a well-known lama and the lineage holder of the Latri lineage. Further education came from Tsultrim Nyima Rinpoche, the lama of Dorpatan Monastery in Nepal. Rinpoche later entered sMenri Monastery in Dolanji, India, the main monastery of the Bön religion and education. There, he was taught by His Holiness, Lungtok Tonpai

Nyima Rinpoche, the 33rd sMenri Trizin (abbot); His Eminence, Yongdzin Tenzin Namdak Rinpoche, the Lopon (head teacher) of all Bön education; and master Lharam Geshe Yundrung Namgyal, a teacher of the Bön Dialectic School at sMenri.

Rinpoche has taught Bön teachings in the U.S., Europe, and Asia since 1990. Rinpoche is an immensely respected geshe, monk, and teacher throughout the world for his authoritative, compassionate, and engaging teaching of Bön, and his ceaseless service to Bön.

Rinpoche was one of the earliest Tibetan Bön monks to teach Bön in the United States. Rinpoche has adhered strictly to the authentic Yungdrung Bön texts and teachings as passed down for thousands of years. He is the author of *Opening the Door to Bön*, the premier guide to the Dzogchen ngondro practices for Western students of Bön.

With the blessing of His Holiness, the 33rd sMenri Trizin, in 1988, Rinpoche founded, and is the President of, the Bön Children's Home in Dolanji, India, which provides housing, clothing, food, and education for orphaned and underprivileged Bön children from northern India, Nepal, Bhutan, and Sikkim. This is the first institute of its kind to provide a full-fledged education from kindergarten to grade 12, as well as continuing education opportunities, for Bön children.

Rinpoche is the founder and Spiritual Director of Yeru Bön Center (headquartered in Minneapolis, with a branch in Los Angeles); Yeru Canada; Shen Chen Ling Bön Center in Minsk (Belarus); Sharza Ling Institute in Poland (with headquarters in

Poznan, Warsaw, and the Sharza Retreat Center (*gomdra*) in Pyszki Kozalkin, Poland); the Bön Shen Ling Center in Moscow; the Bön Shen Drup De Center in Kharkow, Ukraine; and Gyerpung Drubdhe in Donetsk, Ukraine.

# A Short History of Bön

Yungdrung Bön (Tibetan for "Eternal Bön"), also known simply as Bön, is Tibet's indigenous religion. According to Bön's own textual accounts, Bön has more than 18 thousand years of history. Bön originated in the kingdom of Olmo Lung Ring. Bön was founded by Tonpa Shenrab. Tonpa Shenrab was born a prince of Olmo Lung Ring, the son of Yab Gyalbön Thoedkar and Yum Yochi Gyalzhadma, at the Palace of Khar Barpo Sogyed in the kingdom of Olmo Lung Ring. He accomplished the state of enlightenment and spread the teachings of Eternal Bön.

Bön gradually spread to Zhang Zhung, an ancient kingdom that was located in the Mt. Kailash area in the upper region of Tibet. Bön became the religion of Tibet. Tibetans were deeply connected and devoted to Bön and its teachings. Bön was in their blood and hearts until the eighth century, when Buddhism, originating in India, came to Tibet and forcibly displaced Bön as the religion of Tibet.

## Olmo Lung Ring

Olmo Lung Ring is the birthplace of Tonpa Shenrab and is the pure land of the enlightened ones. It is located to the west of Tibet but is not reachable by ordinary people. One can only reach it after removing their defilements and clearing their impure karmic traces.

Olmo Lung Ring has three sections: the outer, middle, and inner. It has four main palaces and many cities, temples, and gardens. It is circled by lakes and snow-covered mountains that form the outer boundary. This outer boundary is the place where Tonpa Shenrab shot his arrow of light and rays to make the arrow path of light (*woeser dhalam*) during his first and only trip to Tibet.

In the center of Olmo Lung Ring is the mountain comprised of a stack of nine yungdrung swastikas (*yungdrung dgu tsek kyi ri*). From the base of this mountain, four holy rivers arise, flowing in four directions. Each river flows from rock formations shaped like the mouth of an animal: one formation looks like an elephant, one like a horse, one like a peacock, and one like a lion.

The name *Olmo Lung Ring* means "The Unborn Source of the Teachings of Love and Compassion." *Ol* means "unborn," or "primordial;" *mo* means "the source of all;" *lung* means "the place of the oral transmission of teachings;" and *ring* means "extending love and compassion."

# Tonpa Shenrab

Tonpa Shenrab was born in a palace called Khar Barpo Sogyed in the Year of the Rat, on the full moon of the first month of the Tibetan Lunar calendar, 18,036 years ago. His birth was heralded with many auspicious signs. The newborn baby was examined, was seen to have perfection in all his qualities, and had the perfect signs of the enlightened ones. He was given the name Tonpa Shenrab Miwo Kunle Nampar Gyalwa, or as he is more commonly known, Tonpa Shenrab, by a priest from the *Dramse* (Sanskrit *Brahmin*) caste.

## Tonpa Shenrab's Teachings

Tonpa Shenrab's teachings are divided into three major topics, known as *khorlo rimpa sum*, "turning the three wheels (of Bön)."

*Khorlo Dangpo*, the "First Wheel of Teaching," concerns *rigpi negna*, "the five major Tibetan sciences," and *thegpa rimpa gu*, "the nine successive ways" of Bön. The teachings of the first wheel mainly emphasize *kunzob dhenpa*, "relative truth."

*Khorlo Barpa*, the "Second Wheel of Teaching," concerns mainly *dhenpa nyi*, "both relative and ultimate truth." This second wheel of teaching deals with understanding the reality of cyclic existence (Tibetan *khorwa*; Sanskrit *samsara*) on the relative level, and then to implement that knowledge in everyday life to make life more meaningful and productive. Gradually, one develops an understanding of absolute truth.

*Khorlo Thama*, the "Third Wheel of Teaching," emphasizes ultimate truth, and is mainly focused on discovering the true nature of all phenomena and developing the wisdom of realization of reality. This is the key to cutting off ignorance, which is the root of suffering.

Tonpa Shenrab's whole life, from his birth until his attainment of Sanggye ("enlightenment," or "final accomplishment,") was dedicated to turning these three wheels of Bön teachings.

Tonpa Shenrab founded the Dzogchen teachings, and their goal is to realize self-awareness.

## Renouncing Worldly Life

At the age of 31, Tonpa Shenrab renounced his princely and family life, and left his palace to follow a path of spiritual journey. Because Tonpa Shenrab realized the meaninglessness of khorwa and the suffering of sentient beings in cyclic existence, he developed unconditional compassion for all beings and was determined to free them all from the ocean of suffering. At the same time, the awareness of intense renunciation from khorwa arose in his mind. He realized that he could only attain his goal of freeing sentient beings from khorwa by attaining the state of enlightenment. Therefore, he decided to become a monk. He cut off his own hair and generously offered his princely robes, precious gems, and ornaments to all beings.

In return for this great deed of virtue and renunciation, his compassion towards all beings and the commitment to enter the path of liberation to liberate all beings, the Enlightened Ones of the

Ten Directions empowered him. They bestowed on him seven new robes and the six necessary utility objects for a monk's day-to-day survival. He also received his spiritual name, which was Tonpa Tritsug Gyalwa, after becoming a monk.

This is the origin and authentic source of the Bön monastic lineage and monastic dress. This lineage and tradition of Bön monks' dress, and the tradition of giving a spiritual name after joining the monastic community, is preserved unbrokenly, despite many challenges, from Tonpa Sherab until today. Tibetan Buddhist monks use the same robes the Bön do, unlike Indian Buddhist monks.

## Tonpa Shenrab's Visit to Tibet

One of Tonpa Shenrab's contemporaries was a *dhud* (demon) named Khyabpa Lagring, who always opposed Tonpa's deeds. On one occasion, Khyabpa stole Tonpa's seven horses from Olmo Lung Ring and took them all the way to Tibet, to Kongpo, and hid them there.

That was his immediate reason to visit Tibet—to rescue his horses. But, it was also the right time to bring Tibetans to the path of Bön teaching and to protect them from continually falling into the impure path of animal sacrifice. At that time, the people of Tibet lacked the knowledge and understanding of the right spiritual path of nonviolence and warm-hearted compassion. Instead, they used animal sacrifices for the sake of temporal benefit. Tonpa Shenrab visited Tibet, because it was the right time to bring the Tibetan people to the spiritual path of enlightenment.

So, he miraculously made a pathway through the snow-covered mountains by shooting an arrow and opening a clear path, known as the *woeser dhalam,* or "arrow path," to enter Tibet via the Zhang Zhung kingdom, and then to the Kongpo Valley, an important part of Tibet.

## Kongpo Bön Ri – The First Teachings in Tibet

Kongpo Bön Ri ("The Holy Mountain of Bön") is located east of Lhasa. It was at Kongpo Bön Ri that Tonpa found his seven horses and subdued the demon who stole them. At the same time, he introduced the fundamental teachings of Bön, specifically: the teachings of the *sang,* (smoke offerings); the teachings about the five colored prayer flags to balance the five elements of our body; ceremonies using *torma* and *tsog* offerings, which use red colored foods instead of animal sacrifices, *chang* (a Tibetan barley beer), and fresh black tea with blessed herbs instead of blood sacrifice; as well as prayers and meditation practices to satisfy local negative spirits so the people would be left in peace.

Tonpa Shenrab also taught Tibetans to practice non-violence, love, and compassion instead of sacrificing in the name of healing or temporal benefit. He taught that sacrifice is unethical and not a solution to overcoming the challenges of life.

This is why, in every spiritual community of Tibetans, you will see prayer flags and *sang* smoke offerings, ransom rituals, and virtuous deeds based on the teachings that originated from Tonpa Shenrab. Tonpa Shenrab did not teach any higher or advanced teachings on his trip to Tibet, because he saw that the Tibetans did not yet have the capacity to understand the higher teachings. But he blessed Tibet with prayers and prophesized that in future the complete Bön doctrine would spread all over Tibet.

He also empowered a specific rock, called *Kunsang Thugka* ("Heart of Kuntu Zangpo"), with many of his holy objects, including his own tooth, which turned itself into a holy conch shell in the center of the Bön mountain, Kongpo Bön Ri.

Tonpa Shenrab also blessed five secret caves, one in each of the four directions and one in the center, of the holy mountain Kongpo Bön Ri. Theses caves still exist, and practitioners use them for their retreats.

There are also four self-originated rocks shaped like thrones in the four directions. These too were blessed by his energy, and many secret syllables appeared by themselves, without any human effort, on these rocks.

### Enlightenment (Leaving His Physical Body on Earth)

At the age of 82, Tonpa Shenrab showed us the truth of the impermanence and uncertainty of life. He left his physical body on the earth, and unified his mind into the primordial sate of Kuntu Zangpo, on the new moon of the tenth month of the Water Rabbit year in the Tibetan calendar. Because Tonpa Shenrab was beyond the cyclic conditions of karma, he was in full control of his life and could live as long as he wanted to. But by leaving his physical body, he showed us unawakened beings the path of realization, which is cutting off grasping at the concept of permanence. He showed us that death may appear at any time, that we can live a more meaningful life if we are free from grasping at material objects, and that we should instead develop the wisdom of self-realization.

## His Successor, Mucho Demdrug

Before he passed away, Tonpa Shenrab empowered Mucho Demdrug and appointed him as *Dhungsob*, his successor. Tonpa Shenrab told him, "You have equal power, qualities, wisdom, and knowledge as me. Therefore, transcend down from the pure land of the gods to continue my teachings."

Tonpa Shenrab specifically advised Mucho Demdrug to collect all his life's teachings and categorize them. So, Mucho formed a *dhu khor chusum* team of thirteen disciples to collect all Tonpa Shenrab's teachings and organized them into 178-volumes, known as *Ka Rinpoche, Oral Teachings of Tonpa Shenrab*. The *Ka Rinpoche* is still in existence today.

## Zamling Khepi Gyendrug, "The Six Great Scholars who are the Ornaments of the World."

Mucho Demdrug had six successors, known as the "Six Great Scholars who are the Ornaments of the World." One was from each of the neighboring countries. They were:

| | |
|---|---|
| From Tagzig: | Mutsa Tahe |
| From Trom: | Serthog Chejam |
| From Gesar: | Ngampa Chering |
| From Menyag: | Chetsa Kharbu |

From India:          Lhadag Ngagdrol

From China:         Legtang Mangpo

These six great scholars translated Bön texts into their native language and spread the Bön teaching in their native land, and then gradually into many other countries, including Zhang Zhung and Tibet.

## Later History of Bön

### Discrimination Against Bön in Tibet

When Tonpa Shenrab made his first and only visit to the Kongpo Valley of Tibet, it was the beginning of the history of Bön in Tibet. Then, gradually, Tonpa Shenrab's prophecy that the complete Bön teachings would flourish in Tibet in the future came true.

From the First Royal King of Tibet, Nyatri Tsenpo, and his son, Mutri Tsenpo, the second king of Tibet, and for thirty-eight royal generations, Bön spread all over Tibet and was the only religion in Tibet at the time. But, by the end of the seventh century, and particularly in the eighth century, a new religion called Buddhism was brought from India to Tibet. This began the darkest period for Bön and Bönpos.

Countless numbers of historical and holy objects were destroyed. Many Bön text were either converted, had names changed, were burned in fire, or were buried in the foundations of Buddhist stupas and temples. Many Bön masters and devotees were killed. During this period, many Bönpos in central Tibet made the sacrifice of not giving up their Bön heritage and were forced to live in fear. But in the outlying and border areas of Kham, Amdo, and Gyarong, and also some of the Himalayan regions, many of the Bön practices were preserved.

### Bön Still Exists and is Well Preserved Today

Today, Bön exists in all three regions of Tibet, as well as in Nepal, Bhutan, India, and many foreign countries. Many of the monasteries and *drubdra* (retreat centers) in Tibet continue to train the younger generation in the traditional ways and give them the authentic three transmissions of Wang, Lung, and Tri to preserve the unbroken lineage of Bön teachings.

In many Bön centers in foreign countries, Rinpoches and geshes are putting in great efforts to teach Bön, in order to preserve its uniqueness and to contribute Bön's wisdom to benefit their communities.

## The Importance of the Three Transmissions (*Wang Lung Tri Sum*)

In the Bön tradition, when studying a particular teaching, it is very important to receive the three transmissions from authentic and authorized Rinpoches or geshes, who themselves received the transmission and are authorized to pass it on to other students or devotees.

# Wang

The word *wang* means "power" or authority. In this case, it means that once you have received a wang from a Rinpoche or other teacher, the teacher is transmitting to you the power of the deity's body, speech, mind, and energy. This removes negative karmic impurities, opens your inner wisdom of realization, and awakens your unawakened mind to connect you with the particular deity of the practice you are doing. If a student receives the wang, it means he or she is empowered to practice the teaching. The teacher may, but not necessarily, give the student the authority to teach the practice and to give a wang transmission of empowerment of the practice to others.

# Lung

The *lung* is the oral transmission, read by the teacher. The lung provides a karmic connection between the student, the teacher, and the source of the lineage of the particular teaching. The lung is meant to bless as well strengthen the quality of practice, the devotion to Bön, and the protection of the student.

# Tri

The *tri* is the teaching itself. *Tri* means receiving the teaching with instructions from a qualified teacher, so the student receives a clear understanding. The tri opens the wisdom of realization, deepens spirituality, and shows how to implement the teaching in everyday life. The tri also confirms the value of meditation and opens a warm heart and compassionate mind towards all beings.

## The History of Termas

The term *terma* generally means a rediscovered hidden treasure. There are two types of *terma*. The first is a *gongter*, or "mind treasure." The second is a *sater*, or "earth treasure," although it is not limited only to the earth but can be recovered from the rocks, ground, water, stupas, and even statues.

The history of *terma* began during the time of Drigun Tsenpo, the eighth king of Tibet. The next period of *terma* was during the persecution in the eighth century. The great *drubshen rigdzins*, "highly realized beings," hid many Bön holy objects to protect them from being destroyed by the king and Buddhist high priests. Later, in the tenth and eleventh centuries, many of these *terma* were rediscovered by a *terton*, persons who found these hidden treasures. The best known of the *tertons* was Shenchen Luga, who revived the Bön system of teaching and traditions. These were gradually spread throughout Tibet again and exist to this day.

## The Preservation of Bön In Exile Today

When Tibet was invaded in 1959, many Tibetans, both Bönpo and Buddhist, fled to Nepal, Bhutan, India, and some Western countries. Living in exile, the Bönpos were a minority, struggling in everyday life but with great willpower and determination to protect and preserve Bön.

A small group of Bön devotees, mostly from the Tewa and Jadhur regions of upper Tibet, settled in Dhorpatan, in northwest Nepal, one of the earliest Tibetan exile settlements. There, Sherab Lodoe, His Holiness the 32nd sMenri Trizin, established the Tashi Gegye Thaten Ling Monastery in 1961. His Holiness the 32nd sMenri Trizin Sherab Lodoe delegated to Tsultrim Nyima Rinpoche the responsibility to lead the monastery, assisted by Akhu Tsultrim Gyaltsen, Latri Kuchung Gyaltsen Nyima (also known as Tewa Lama), Akhu Tenpa Gyaltsen, Genchen Yeshe Sangpo, Genchen Lodoe Tendar, Genchen Adam Tsering, many other Bönpo elders, and some of the original monks from sMenri Monastery in Tibet. Then, the monastery was blessed with the consecration by His Holiness the 32nd sMenri Trizin and lamas who were present then.

Several other groups of Bönpos were scattered throughout northern India, many on the Manali Road construction site in Himachal Pradesh, India, under the guidance and blessing of His Holiness Yungdrung Ling Khen Chen and His Eminence Senior sMenri Ponlob Sangye Tenzin Rinpoche. His Eminence Yongzin Rinpoche was able to acquire some land in the village of Dolanji in Himachal Pradesh and established a Bön settlement in 1968 called New Thobgyal Bön Settlement, registered under the name of the Tibetan Bön Foundation. The senior monks at Dolanji, including His Holiness Yungdrung Ling Khenchen, the senior sMenri Lopon His Eminence Sanggye Tenzin Rinpoche, His Eminence Yongzin

Rinpoche, and many other Rinpoches determined to select the 33rd sMenri Trizin. As a result of the traditional selection process, Sanggye Tenzin Jongdhong became the 33rd sMenri Trizin. He built the temple and the Pal Shenten sMenri Ling monastery in 1969, which became the Mother Monastery of Bön in exile. sMenri Monastery serves as the central education of Bön, and there reside many monks, geshes, and Rinpoches from Tibet, Nepal, Bhutan, and different parts of India.

Another monastery, Za Mongyal Yungdrung Ling Monastery, was founded in 1974 by Lama Trinley Gyatso. It was constructed at the Kham Lingtsang Society in Deradun, in the state of Uttar Khand in northern India. This monastery was originally in the Kham Lingtsang kingdom. The land was offered by a Prince of Lingtsang (Lingtsang Gyaltsey). The head of this monastery is His Eminence the 7th Kundrol Namkha Wangyal Rinpoche. The current main temple, including the interior and outer structure, was built by Latri Khenpo Nyima Dakpa Rinpoche, with the consecration of His Holiness the 33rd sMenri Trizin. Then, Latri Khenpo Nyima Dakpa Rinpoche handed the completed temple over to Kundrol Namkha Wangyal Rinpoche.

In Rabangla, in Sikkim, the Zhu Rizhing Yungdrung Kundrag Ling Monastery was founded in 1984 by Lama Yungdrung Tsultrim. The new head lama is Khenpo Geshe Nyima Senge.

Triten Norbutse Monastery was founded in 1987 by His Eminence Yongzin Lopon Tenzin Namdak Rinpoche, at Ichangu Gaon, Raniban, Katmandhu, Nepal. It became one of the most important educational centers of the Bön in exile.

Ratna sMenling (the only Bön nunnery in exile) was founded in 2001 by His Holiness the 33rd sMenri Trizin, Lungtok Tenpe Nyima, the Spiritual Head of Bön at the New Thogyal Bön settlement, Dolanji, Himachal Pradesh, India. This is the first time in history that sMenri offered nuns the chance to study at the dialectic school (*shedra*) and to obtain a geshe degree equal to that of monks.

A small Bön temple called Yundrung Lhatse Gon was founded in 2002 by sMenri Geshe Lungrig Nyima at Choglamsar, Ladhak, India.

Shen Gyi Sangnag Gomdrub Ling (Yogi Temple) was founded in 2005 by His Holiness the 33rd sMenri Trizin, Lungtok Tenpe Nyima, the Spiritual Head of Bön at the New Thogyal Bön settlement, Dolanji, Himachal Pradesh, India.

Another monastery was built in Sikkim, named Sog Yungdrung Ling, founded in 2013 by Khenpo Yontent Gyatso, in Yanggang, Sikkim.

In Bhutan, for many years a group of Bön devotees have maintained a small gompa of Sidpe Gyalmo (Sidgyal Gompa). The acting lama of this gompa is Geshe Samdup Nyima, from sMenri Monastery.

Made in the USA
San Bernardino, CA
30 April 2020